PENGUIN CLASSICS

THE CONSOLATION OF PHILOSOPHY

ADVISORY EDITOR: BETTY RADICE

Ancius Boethius (*c*. A.D. 480–524), the Roman philosopher, has been called one of the last authentic representatives of the classical world, in both his life and writings. He came of a family which had held office in the decaying Western empire. He was Consul in 510, and a trusted political adviser to Theodoric, the Ostrogoth. Later he became involved in a conspiracy and was imprisoned and executed at Ravenna. The historical importance of his work was immense, because it was only through Boethius's translations that the knowledge of Aristotle survived in the West. He also wrote commentaries on Cicero, text-books on arithmetic and music, and a number of works on theology. His works were chosen for translation by Alfred the Great and he was one of the most influential Latin authors for the next thousand years.

V. E. Watts was born in 1938 and read classics and English at Merton College, Oxford, and did a year of postgraduate work at University College, London. He is now Senior Lecturer in the Department of English Language and Medieval Literature at Durham University. His publications include articles and reviews and an edition of 'On trees and herbs', Book 17 of the medieval encyclopaedia *On the Properties of Things* by Bartholomaeus Anglicus.

BOETHIUS

The Consolation of Philosophy

*

TRANSLATED WITH AN
INTRODUCTION BY
V. E. WATTS

PENGUIN BOOKS

Penguin Books Ltd, Harmondsworth, Middlesex, England
Viking Penguin Inc., 40 West 23rd Street, New York, New York 10010, U.S.A.
Penguin Books Australia Ltd, Ringwood, Victoria, Australia
Penguin Books Canada Limited, 2801 John Street, Markham, Ontario, Canada L3R 1B4
Penguin Books (N.Z.) Ltd, 182–190 Wairau Road, Auckland 10, New Zealand

—

This translation first published 1969
Reprinted 1976, 1978, 1980, 1981, 1982, 1984, 1986, 1987

—

Copyright © V. E. Watts, 1969
All rights reserved

—

Printed and bound in Great Britain by
Cox & Wyman Ltd, Reading
Set in Monotype Bembo

CONTENTS

INTRODUCTION

I. Introductory

THE *Consolation of Philosophy* has been many things to many men. In a much quoted phrase Gibbon described it as 'a golden volume not unworthy of the leisure of Plato or Tully', though he found its philosophy ineffectual.[1] The Middle Ages did not find it so, and provided the *Consolation* with a long series of translators, commentators and imitators. King Alfred turned it into Old English for the education and enjoyment of his Anglo-Saxon subjects, and Chaucer and John the Chaplain into Middle English; Notker Labeo and Peter von Kastl turned it into medieval German, and Simun de Fraisne, Jean de Meung and others into Old French. There were versions in Greek and Middle Dutch, in Old Provençal, in Italian and in Spanish; later an English queen – Elizabeth I – turned her hand to Englishing the *Consolation*; and the tradition of translation still continues, though most of us need rather longer than the twenty-four or twenty-seven hours in which she is reputed to have completed her version.

Boethius stands at the crossroads of the Classical and Medieval worlds. 'No philosopher,' wrote Richard Morris, 'was so bone of the bone and flesh of the flesh of Middle-Age writers as Boethius. Take up what writer you will, and you find not only the sentiments, but the very words of the distinguished old Roman.'[2] The extent and diffusion of Boethius' influence have been traced elsewhere.[3] In the case of the

1. *The Decline and Fall of the Roman Empire*, ed. J. B. Bury, London, 1898, IV, p. 201.

2. *Chaucer's Translation of Boethius de Consolatione Philosophiae*, ed. R. Morris, Early English Text Society, Extra Series V, 1868, p. 2.

3. See the full treatment given in H. F. Stewart, *Boethius – An Essay*, Edinburgh/London, 1891, and H. R. Patch, *The Tradition of Boethius; A Study of his*

Consolation it was due, no doubt, to the fact that here Boethius was attempting something other than a formal philosophical treatise. In the confines of prison he was no longer concerned with the minute details and technicalities of argument, but with the consolation to be gained from a broad and general philosophical meditation. In retrospect, though I do not think this aspect of his work would have occurred to Boethius himself, it is perhaps justified to regard him as 'the divine popularizer'.[4]

This popular quality was doubly important. Firstly, along with the fact that Boethius was no mean poet, it made the *Consolation* available to the poets. In Britain it inspired the author of *The Kingis Quair* to meditate on the wheel of Fortune and write his remarkable little poem; while almost all the passages of philosophical reflection of any length in the works of Chaucer can be traced to Boethius. And in Italy, to cite only one other example, Dante set Boethius among the twelve lights in the heaven of the Sun, calling him

> That joy who strips the world's hypocrisies
> Bare to whoever heeds his cogent phrases:[5]

for along with Cicero's *De Amicitia*, the words of Boethius, he tells us, provided him with his greatest consolation after the death of Beatrice. The *Paradise* actually ends with a reminiscence of Boethius' *caelo imperitans amor* – 'the love that moves the sun and other stars'[6] – and *The Divine Comedy* as a whole could be regarded as a great elaboration of Boethius' concept of the ascent of the soul to the contemplation of the mind of God and its return to its true home or *patria* in the scheme of the universe.

Importance in Medieval Culture, New York/Oxford, 1935: also C. S. Lewis's stimulating little sketch in *The Discarded Image*, Cambridge, 1964.

4. C. S. Lewis, *The Allegory of Love*, Oxford, 1936, p. 46.

5. *The Divine Comedy: Paradise*, X, 125, translated by Dorothy L. Sayers and Barbara Reynolds, Penguin Books, 1962.

6. XXXIII, 145: cf. *Cons.* II poem 8 l.29.

Secondly, the broad scope and gentle tone of the *Consolation* produced 'the book of most serene and kindly wisdom that the Middle Ages knew'.[7] It was the book that 'saved the thought of the Middle Ages', wrote W. P. Ker in his short but lucid account of Boethius.[8] 'The beauty of it, which lifts it far above the ordinary run of reflections on mortality, is that it restores a Platonic tradition, or even something older and simpler in Greek philosophy, at a time when simplicity and clearness of thought were about to be overwhelmed in the medieval confusion. ... His protection was always to be had by anyone who found the divisions and distinctions of the schools too much for him. In the *Consolation of Philosophy* there was a place of outlook from which the less valuable matters sank back into their proper place, and the real outlines of the world were brought into view. ... There can be little question that Boethius, more than any other philosophic author, helped the great Schoolmen to retain a general comprehensive view of the world as a whole, in spite of the distractions of their minute inquiries.'

II. Boethius' Life and Writings

Anicius Manlius Severinus Boethius, born in or about A.D. 480, was a member of an ancient and aristocratic family, the *gens Anicia*. Since their conversion to Christianity in the fourth century – unusually early for an established and conservative family – the Anicii had risen to great power and wealth, and among his ancestors and kinsmen, besides many consuls, Boethius could number two emperors and a pope. His father himself had followed an honourable career of public service, attaining to the consulship under the barbarian king Odoacer in 487, but dying while his son was still a boy.

7. Helen Waddell, *The Wandering Scholars*, Penguin Books, 1954, p. 26.
8. *The Dark Ages*, Edinburgh/London, 1923, pp. 107 ff.

Boethius was brought up in the home of another pàtrician family, that of the famous Quintus Aurelius Memmius Symmachus, consul in 485, and later Prefect of Rome and Head of the Senate. It was Symmachus who introduced Boethius to the worlds of literature and philosophy, and of him and of his daughter, Rusticiana, whom he later married, Boethius speaks in the *Consolation* with reverence and admiration.

According to his kinsman, Ennodius, Boethius was something of an infant prodigy and early showed an unusual passion for study. His education, whether at Athens or not, was of the highest quality, and as a young man Boethius was master of all the liberal arts, from rhetoric to logic and astronomy.[9]

Both Ennodius and Cassiodorus – another kinsman of Boethius and a cabinet-minister of Theodoric the Ostrogoth – speak of Boethius' eloquence, his perfection of style, and his perfect command of Greek – an accomplishment of growing rarity at the end of the fifth century.

At an early age and in a manner unknown to us, Boethius came to the notice of the great Ostrogothic king Theodoric who had defeated Odoacer and murdered him in 493. Theodoric, in the most flattering terms commissioned him to construct a water clock and sundial for Gundobad, king of the Burgundians, and to choose a lyre player for Clovis, king of the Franks.[10] He was also employed to investigate a case of alleged debasement of the coinage by the paymaster of the life-guards, and in 510 he was made consul without companion. Thus at the age of thirty he held what was traditionally the most illustrious of all the Roman offices – dignities denied to the majority of men at any age[11] – although in the days of Theodoric the consulate was of little more than titular importance.

9. cf. *Consolation* I, poem 2.
10. *The Letters of Cassiodorus*, translated by Thomas Hodgkin, London, 1886, pp. 169 and 193.
11. *Cons.* II, 3.

Later – the year is not known – Theodoric made him *magister officiorum*, a position which involved him in onerous and responsible duties. He became head of the whole civil service and chief of the palace officials. And then in 522 came the moment which Boethius still regarded even in prison as the hour of his greatest happiness, the day when his two boys were appointed consuls together. It was a unique honour accorded to the father and implies his joint recognition by both Theodoric and the Emperor in Constantinople.

The years immediately following his own consulship are obscure. But it is during this period that he must have pursued the studies he had begun in the house of Symmachus, for the duties of *magister officiorum*, involving, as they must have done, prolonged absences from Rome at the court in Verona or Ravenna, would have parted him from his library and allowed him little time for his impassioned pursuit of the philosophy which he considered his *summum vitae solamen* – his chief solace in life.[12]

It was not in the forefront of public life but in the study and treatment of all the branches of philosophy that Boethius' true calling lay. And he pursued this aim with a single-minded dedication and methodical steadfastness which only the recollection of his childhood precocity renders less than astounding. It is here that the real Boethius is clearest to view, the scholarly character, the calm almost leisured approach to his self-appointed task. It was not the retreat of an escapist from the acute feeling of the insignificance of the once proud offices of the Roman state, but the deliberate plan of the dedicated student to give his fellow countrymen the basis they still lacked for a truly scholarly study of philosophy. 'Boethius saw himself,' Campenhausen writes, 'as the schoolmaster of the West.'[13]

---

12. *De syllogismo hypothetico I*, Migne, LXIV, 831B.
13. *The Fathers of the Latin Church*, translated by Manfred Hoffman, London, 1964, p. 289.

I wish [Boethius says] to translate the whole work of Aristotle, so far as it is accessible to me, into the Roman idiom and conscientiously offer his complete utterances in the Latin tongue. Everything Aristotle ever wrote on the difficult art of logic, on the important realm of moral experience, and on the exact comprehension of natural objects, I shall translate in the correct order. Moreover, I shall make all this comprehensible by interpretative explanations. I should also like to translate all Plato's Dialogues, and likewise explain them, and thus present them in a Latin version. When this is accomplished, I will furthermore not shrink from proving that the Aristotelian and Platonic conceptions in every way harmonize, and do not, as is widely supposed, completely contradict each other. I will show, moreover, that they are in agreement with one another at the philosophically decisive points. This is the task to which I will dedicate myself, so far as life and leisure for work are vouchsafed to me. I know that this will be as useful as it is laborious, and that it needs the assistance of those powers which are ever alien to envy and jealousy.[14]

Boethius did not fulfil his plan, but he did finish translations of Porphyry's *Introduction to the Categories of Aristotle* – to serve as a student's introduction – and Aristotle's works on logic. These included the *De Interpretatione*, the *Topics*, the *Prior* and *Posterior Analytics* and the *Sophistical Fallacies*, and it is clear that he also knew Aristotle's *Metaphysics*, *Physics*, *De Generatione et Corruptione*, *De Anima* and *Poetics*. Furthermore he wrote commentaries on Porphyry's *Introduction*, on probably all the works of Aristotle that he translated, and on Cicero's *Topics*. But his philosophical work was not entirely one of transmission: he also wrote five independent works of his own on logic.

The historical importance of all this work was immense, because it was only through Boethius' translations of his logic that the knowledge of Aristotle survived in the West. By his careful literal translation of philosophical terms Boethius created a new philosophical vocabulary for the medieval

14. *Commentary on Aristotle's De Interpretatione*, quoted by Campenhausen, op. cit., pp. 285–6.

schoolmen. And in his commentaries he offered them a model for their own commentaries on Aristotle. The great medieval debate between Nominalists and Realists has its seeds in a passage in Boethius' commentary on Porphyry. 'The last of the Romans; the first of the scholastics':[15] the formula summarizes Boethius' position as the channel through whose precise and organized systematization philosophy passed from the ancient world to the academic discussions of Scholasticism.

The liberal arts, too, had value for him, as for St Augustine, as a propaedeutic to philosophy. Consequently he wrote treatises – or rather translations of treatises – on arithmetic, on geometry and possibly on astronomy and mechanics. These were important in the development of medieval education; his treatise on music, for instance, remained a textbook at Oxford until the eighteenth century. Boethius also gave us the word *quadrivium*, believing that 'it was impossible to achieve the summit of perfection in the disciplines of philosophy unless one approached this noble wisdom by a kind of fourfold way.'[16]

He is also accredited with five small works or tractates of theology, the authenticity of at least four of which is beyond doubt. They are completely orthodox in doctrine and are important as representing the attempt of a philosopher primarily interested in logic to apply the methods of philosophy to the support of a body of revealed truth which exists in its own right. In his application of logical methods and the terminology of Aristotle to theological problems Boethius clearly stands out again as a forerunner of the scholastics.

All this activity forms the intellectual background of his last great work, the work for which above all else he is remembered. And yet it is surrounded by question marks. What were the circumstances of its composition? Why did the trusted right-hand servant of Theodoric fall so abruptly from

15. The origin of this description is traced in Patch, op. cit., p. 127.
16. *De Arithmetica*, Migne LXIII, 1079D.

power? Was Boethius a Christian, and if so why does the *Consolation* lack all reference to the faith that should have been his greatest consolation in the hours of imprisonment and pending death?

Only one of these questions can be answered with certainty. Since the authorship of the *Theological Tractates* – with perhaps one exception – is unimpeachable, and since in any case it would have been impossible for an overt pagan to have risen so high in public life in the early sixth century, scholarship is satisfied that Boethius must have been a Christian. But while the fact of his Christianity cannot be doubted, its quality is still a matter on which there is disagreement. And while the historical facts surrounding his downfall are beyond recall, from Boethius' own words and the testimonies of the times a hypothesis can be constructed.[17]

It must be remembered that since the beginning of the fourth century the Roman Empire had been provided with an Eastern capital at Constantinople, and that since the end of that century it had been governed by the joint rule of a Western and an Eastern emperor. In 476 the barbarian Odoacer deposed the last emperor of the West and sent the Imperial Insignia to Constantinople; in barbarian eyes only a Roman could assume the purple, and Odoacer seems to have been content to preserve the imperial administration in Rome and recognize the Eastern Zeno as sole emperor, in return for the title 'Patricius'.

Thus a loose *modus vivendi* was established between the barbarians and the emperor. In practice Odoacer was an autonomous king; but in theory – and in Roman eyes – he was

17. For an account of the evidence and various views, see H. F. Stewart, op. cit., E. K. Rand, *Founders of the Middle Ages*, Harvard University Press, 1929, M. Cappuyns s.n. 2. Boèce in *Dictionnaire d'Histoire et de Géographie Ecclésiastique*, IX, 1937, and H. M. Barrett, *Boethius: some aspects of his times and work*, Cambridge, 1940. In the account which follows I am chiefly indebted to Campenhausen, op. cit. Cf. also W. C. Bark, *Theodoric vs. Boethius*, in *American Historical Review* XLIX, 1944, pp. 410–26.

regarded as a kind of Viceroy, a servant of the Emperor at Constantinople in a single unified Empire. This system was preserved by Theodoric, king of the Ostrogoths, when he succeeded Odoacer in 493. To the emperor Anastasius he wrote: 'Our royalty is an imitation of yours, a copy of the only Empire on earth.'[18]

A great military leader of a barbaric people, yet educated in the sophisticated circles of the court at Constantinople, Theodoric had all the qualities to impose a firm and peaceful rule upon Italy. Both king of the barbarians and Viceroy of the emperor, he succeeded in establishing the peaceful coexistence of Roman and Goth. The administration was carried on by the Roman civil service, but it was directed by Theodoric's strong and vigorous guidance. To his service he was able to attract Romans of the calibre of Liberius, Cassiodorus and Boethius. Industry prospered, peace reigned, buildings and aqueducts were restored and rebuilt. And the success of Theodoric's rule at home was mirrored by his increasing prestige abroad.

In matters of religion Theodoric was a Christian, but an Arian, a member, like all the Goths, of that heretical sect which believed that the Father and the Son were not 'one substance'. This heresy had split the church, and yet Theodoric found no difficulty in ruling in the city of the Pope and the capital of orthodoxy. He firmly supported complete freedom of worship for all – except pagans – and remained on friendly terms with the orthodox clergy, on one occasion even being invited to arbitrate in a disputed papal election. For the moment the seeds of future suspicion and hostility were dormant.

Boethius' decision to serve as Theodoric's minister involved him, as we have seen, in considerable self-sacrifice. Like Symmachus – himself a scholar with a thorough command of Greek, a writer of history, and a brilliant speaker, a man who

18. Quoted by Donald Bullough in *The Dark Ages*, London, 1965, p. 158.

though he had served the barbarian overlords preserved a certain aloofness and reserve towards them – Boethius too would have preferred a life of study among his books. His decision to enter real politics was dictated by a sense of duty rather than a desire for fame. From his own words we learn that the Platonic ideal of the state governed by philosophers was his inspiration[19] and the lessons of philosophy his guide in the exercise of his offices.[20]

Given such principles of conduct and such disinterested moral rectitude, and given the animosities, the suspicions and deceits, the intrigue and self aggrandizement encountered in political life, it was impossible that Boethius should not make enemies. At first he was successful in opposing Gothic rapaciousness and enjoyed Theodoric's support.[21] But this external circumstances were to change.

In 484 there had been a doctrinal breach between East and West, known, because of the Pope's condemnation of the Byzantine Patriarch Acacius, as the Acacian schism. Insofar as it strengthened his independence of the East, the hostility of the Pope and Italian clergy to Constantinople was not un-welcome to Theodoric; but to those who held the unity of the Empire dear – and this seems to have included the circle around Symmachus to which Boethius and many of the senators belonged and which continuously looked to the East – the breach was deplorable. It is not unlikely that, although as far as can be seen Boethius remained aloof from the battles of ecclesiastical controversy, his theological tractates were meant in some sort as a modest contribution towards solving the dispute. The breach in fact was officially healed in 519 although the controversy did not end at once. Boethius sided with the East and the honour done to him in 522 was perhaps originally proposed by the Emperor.

19. Boethius' favourite Platonic dialogue seems to have been the *Republic*.
20. *Cons.* I, 4.
21. *Cons.*, ibid.

The end of the schism and its aftermath had political as well as theological implications. Not only had the Senate been openly appealed to, but the rapprochement between East and West threatened Theodoric's position: in Roman eyes their true lord was once again the orthodox Emperor, while Theodoric remained an invader and a heretic.

The combination of circumstances led inevitably to Boethius' downfall; he was a man of principle rather than a politician, and his sympathies were firmly on the side of the Empire and its culture rather than with the Gothicizing circle of Cyprian. The time was ripe for his enemy to play upon the already aroused suspicions of the king who had been further incensed by the renewed persecution of Arians in the East.[22] Letters to Constantinople were intercepted in which a senator named Albinus appears to have expressed himself indiscreetly in some way, perhaps in connexion with the recent election of the pro-Eastern Pope John I: and when Boethius tried to dismiss the matter, evidence – whether false, as Boethius claims, or not, we do not know – was produced to implicate him. Was he not the man who had striven against the Goths Conigast and Triguilla and himself written against the Arian heresy?[23] Within a short while he was arrested, condemned and sent into exile to await execution. The senate, overawed by Theodoric, confirmed the sentence and after being cruelly tortured Boethius was bludgeoned to death at Pavia, the place of his exile, in 524 or 525.

The truth of his case will never be known. Boethius' allegiance to the Roman Imperial idea may have seemed consistent to him with his service of the Gothic king; but seen through barbarian eyes it could understandably be viewed as

22. Boethius' opinions of his accusers is not, of course, without bias in *Cons.* I, 4. The picture we get of Cyprian from Cassiodorus is of a gifted and impartial young lawyer, and Opilio too is warmly commended. See *The Letters*, ed. Hodgkin, pp. 289 ff. and 361 ff.

23. In his tractate *On the Catholic Faith*.

treason. At any rate, Theodoric's revenge extended after Boethius' death to include Symmachus and the Pope as well, and before he died old and embittered in 526 his whole policy of peaceful coexistence lay in ruins. Along with it the Roman aristocracy, the proud and ancient offices of state and the whole study of philosophy virtually disappeared, until the latter was rediscovered, long after the attack of Justinian and the invasion of the Lombards, by the ninth-century Carolingian renaissance.

On 15 December 1883 the Sacred Congregation of Rites in Rome in concert with the Bishop of Pavia approved the local cult of St Severinus Boethius. The cult is as old at least as the ninth though not popular until the thirteenth century when Dante knew of Boethius' resting place in the church of San Pietro in Cielo d'Oro in Pavia. Peter Abelard and the Middle Ages may have been right to venerate Boethius along with Symmachus and Pope John as orthodox martyrs of Arianism, but the modern view tends to regard this as too great an oversimplification.

III. *The Consolation of Philosophy*

Between his condemnation and his execution there was a period of delay during which Boethius was imprisoned at Pavia. The conditions of this imprisonment we do not know, but he had sufficient freedom to meditate on and write the *Consolation*. Some have thought that he must have had access to his books in the writing; but the many casual references, recollections and quotations scattered throughout the work – not only from philosophers, but also from the great literary figures like Catullus, Claudian, Euripides, Homer, Juvenal, Lucan, Menander, Ovid, Seneca (especially his Tragedies), Sophocles, Statius and Virgil – are scarcely matters for wonder in a man whose youth was devoted to avid reading and in an age when the memory was commonly keener and more retentive than in our own.

We must, then, in the absence of firm evidence to the contrary, believe Boethius that he wrote in prison, alone, under the shadow of eventual execution, unaided except by the power of his own memory and genius.

In form the *Consolation* belongs to the ancient genre of the *consolatio,* a branch of the diatribe which in pagan Greece and Rome was especially the province of philosophy. It was cultivated by all the schools of philosophy, and by the time of Seneca the science of *consolatio* had become, in the words of J. Martha,[24] 'a kind of moral medication. ... It was only necessary to open the drawer corresponding to the illness in question in order to find at once the remedies most appropriate for a cure.' This is the source of the extended medical metaphor used by Philosophy and of the diagnosis of the true nature of Boethius' sickness in Book I. It is the source too of the examination of Fortune, of the use of historical examples, and of the popular eclectic philosophy of commonplace *solacia* which underlies a good deal of Book II and which includes the memorable passage of prose which demonstrates, after the manner of Cicero in the *Dream of Scipio*, how trivial and provincial earthly fame and glory are.[25]

But the *Consolation* is a skilled fusion of more than one genre. In part it approximates to the monologue, and in part it imitates the dialectic of the Platonic dialogue. The whole, in fact, is cast in the form of a particular type of dialogue, the sacred dialogue, in which the author describes how some divine spirit or power, at first unknown to him, appears and reveals to him some portion of hidden wisdom, as, for instance, in the second book of Esdras in the Apocrypha, ch. 3 ff.

The combination of apocalyptic dialogue and Menippean Satire – a form of composition, Greek in origin and later

24. Quoted by C. Favez in *La Consolation Latine Chrétienne*, Paris, 1937, p. 11.
25. *Cons.* II, 7.

latinized, in which sections of prose alternate with verse –[26] was already in existence before Boethius wrote. The most famous example was Martianus Capella's extraordinary *Marriage of Philology and Mercury:* the knowledge of this book may not have offered Boethius much help, but it may have been the inspiration for his choice of the literary form which he raised to greater heights than it had ever before achieved.

In the *Consolation,* then, there is a skilful combination of varied literary forms. And a similar, or greater exhibition of literary skill is displayed in the thirty-nine poems which intersperse and enliven the discourse. Their presence is integral and their purpose varied. They act as a relief from the concentration of the argument while the patient is still weak; but as he grows stronger and the argument more complex, their occurrence is less frequent. (It is not by accident that the *Consolation* begins with verse and ends with prose.) Sometimes they are used to summarize or even advance the discussion. And sometimes their function is not unlike that of the chorus in a Greek tragedy, offering a gnomic comment and lending distance and perspective to the intense and personal progress of the dialogue.

There have been varying opinions of their poetic merit. A ninth-century writer thought that Boethius was the equal of Cicero in his prose and of Virgil in his poetry, and the great Scaliger considered the poetry divine.[27] On the other hand Hermann Usener saw in the metrical interludes the voice of a child of the sixth century compared with the maturity of the proses, and to W. P. Ker 'the verse of the *Consolation* is that of

26. The word *satire* – Latin *satura* – meant in origin nothing more than 'medley'. As a literary form it is one 'that has no equal for its Protean changes of contents throughout its lengthy history. Our English Satire is only one moment in its career.' E. K. Rand, op. cit., p. 163.

27. Barrett, op. cit., p. 165; but the ninth-century judgement is perhaps no more a sober assessment than the conventional panegyric 'outdoing', cf. E. R. Curtius, *European Literature and the Latin Middle Ages,* translated by W. R. Trask, Bollingen Series XXXVI, 1953, pp. 162 ff. Scaliger is quoted by Stewart, op. cit., p. 78.

a prosodist – somewhat too deliberate in the choice and combination of metres, not always quite successful, it may be thought.'[28] Granted that some of the poems are clever without being distinguished, not a few rise to greater heights: I, 5 was already set to music by the ninth century; II, 7 contains the famous reference to the bones of Fabricius; Books III and IV contain a number of good poems including the fine retelling of the story of Orpheus and Eurydice; and no one can fail to be moved by the majestic and magistral poetry of the ninth poem of Book III. This was so famous in the Middle Ages for the reasons given in the note on page 98 that it had its own special commentaries written by Bruno of Corvey and Adalbold of Utrecht. In his prose style, too, Boethius is considerably superior in his simplicity and restraint to the usual elaboration and diffuseness of the prose writers of the time.

In one of his commentaries on Porphyry, Boethius wrote:

This love of wisdom (or philosophy) is the illumination of the intelligent mind by that pure wisdom (defined as the self-sufficient living mind and sole primaeval reason of all things), and is a kind of return and recall to it, so that it seems at once the pursuit of wisdom, the pursuit of divinity and the friendship of that pure mind. So that this wisdom gives to the whole class of minds the reward of its own divinity and returns it to its proper constitution and purity of nature.[29]

Herein lies the philosophical basis of the *Consolation*. Philosophy descends to Boethius from on high (I, 3) and leads him back through various paths to God Himself. Her varying height in I, 1 is symbolic: sometimes she is of average height,

---

28. Op. cit., p. 115. It should be noted that quite a number of the Latin metres used are unique to Boethius. For Usener's view see Rand, op. cit., p.165 and note 55 on p. 319.

29. *In Porphyrium dialogus primus*, Migne, *Patrologia Latina* LXIV 11A, quoted by F. Klingner in *De Boethii Consolatione Philosophiae*, 2. Unveranderte Auflage, Zurich/Dublin, 1966, p. 117.

offering the practical philosophy of Book II; sometimes she pierces the sky leading back to God from Whom she came.

The scheme is undoubtedly Platonic. The turning of the gaze from what is false to what is true (III, 1) and the realization that God is the supreme good (III, 10) is based on the ascent of the soul in the famous allegory of the Cave in the seventh book of the *Republic*. The ascent or education of the soul is like the ascent of a man from a dark cave in which he has been chained since childhood, unable to see more than shadows on the wall. When he is freed he is brought step by step up into the light until he is eventually able to see the sun itself, the Idea of the Good.

But the ascent of the soul is not simply a process of education, it is also one of remembering: and the Platonic basis of the *Consolation* is seen again in the reference to this doctrine of *anamnesis* or recollection in poem 2 of Book III.[30] Here we find a Neoplatonic fusion of concepts not formally associated by Plato: the ascent of the soul is connected with the doctrine of recollection, and both are seen in terms of the turning in upon itself of the soul and its illumination by its own inward light.

The notion of recollection underlies the whole of Book III. Already in chapter 6 of Book I Boethius' condition is diagnosed as due to the loss of the memory of his true nature. His mind dreams of true happiness (III, 1), but like other men his memory is clouded (III, 2). For there is a natural attraction of the soul to the Good, but it is frequently deflected and frustrated along false byways.[31] When, however, Boethius has been brought to the point at which he is ready to turn away from what is false to what is true, the recollection and the ascent which is prayed for in the ninth poem of Book III seem almost to be accomplished by poetic uplift and anticipation in

30. See the note on this poem on p. 109.
31. Cf. F. Copleston, *A History of Philosophy*, I, ch. 20, on the concept of Eros in Plato's *Symposium*.

the sublime closing lines of that poem.[32] By the end of the Book prose draws level with poetry again and Philosophy has shown the true nature of God, though not without a hint in the Orpheus allegory that Boethius may yet lapse into error.

The *Consolation of Philosophy* was written in prison, and, as E. K. Rand has observed, prison-literature often takes the form of a theodicy, an attempt to

> assert eternal Providence
> And Justify the ways of God to men.

We might compare, for instance, Sir Thomas More's *Dialogue of Cumfort against Tribulation,* also written in prison and under the threat of execution. So Boethius' bitter experiences led him into a reconsideration of the nature of happiness. The method he uses is that of Platonic dialectic, the diction and conventions of which he carefully imitates,[33] though the substance of the argument is drawn from a different source, perhaps from St Augustine.[34] To the modern reader this use of dialectic will probably seem the least successful part of the *Consolation.* This is because it tends to treat words as if they had an unchanging value like the symbols of algebra or logic. For this reason the argument at the end of Book III that 'evil is nothing' on the grounds that 'God who can do all things cannot do evil' and that 'what God cannot do is nothing', and the further conclusion that evil men are powerless, will fail to convince. It contains, however, the seeds of further discussion in Book IV.

This Book is what Campenhausen calls 'a detailed theodicy developed in the Platonic spirit'.[35] The first part concerning the strength of the good and weakness of the bad and their rewards and punishment, including the idea that criminals should be treated as sick men, is based on Plato's *Gorgias.* The

32. See Klingner, op. cit., pp. 62-6. 33. See Klingner, op. cit., pp. 75 ff.
34. Ibid., p. 72. 35. Op. cit., p. 304.

...rt, in answer to Boethius' hesitations concerning the ...God's control of the universe, involves Philosophy in a fresh beginning.

Thus chapter 6 marks the end of Socratic dialogue and rhetorical embellishment, the end of Boethius' dependence on Plato and the advance to a higher plane of argument, viz. the exposition of the two aspects of history as Providence – the simple unchanging plan in the mind of God – and Fate – the ever changing distribution in and through time of all the events God has planned in his simplicity. Boethius appears to have combined two ideas; the idea of a mutable Fate governing and revolving all things, which he read of in the treatise *On Providence and Fate* by the fifth-century Neoplatonist Proclus, and the idea, already touched on, at the end of Book III chapter 12, of God as the 'still point of the turning world', an idea he found in the philosophy of Plotinus. The union of the two ideas is perfect. The more the soul frees itself from corporeal things, and thus, according to both Proclus and Plotinus, from Fate,[36] the closer it approaches the stability and simplicity of the place of rest at the centre, which according to Plotinus is God, the hinge of things, or Providence, the source of freedom and consolation for Boethius. This is a brilliant example of what H. R. Patch calls Boethius' 'inspired eclecticism', the skill with which he blends received material from various sources to form a new and harmonious whole.[37]

The poem which follows celebrates in verse the truth which has just been proclaimed, God's benevolent government of the universe, for the question of the presence of evil in the world has its solution in the vision of divine peace. This theme occurs in a number of poems which deal with the problem of how the universe is constituted and offer a generally Platonic answer. First in Book I poem 5 Boethius praises God's

---

36. Cf. Philosophy's argument in Book V, 2.
37. See H. R. Patch, *Fate in Boethius and the Neoplatonists*, in *Speculum*, IV, 1929, pp. 62–72 for details.

government of the universe, but asks why it is withheld from human affairs and why men are subject to the whims of Fortune. He concludes with a prayer which seems to echo the 'Thy will be done in earth as in heaven' of the Lord's Prayer. Then in the last poem of Book II, Philosophy sings of the power of love in the natural world preserving peace and keeping chaos at bay. She answers Boethius by specifically saying that God's government does include human affairs: love makes peace between nations, blesses marriage and cements friendship. But she also implies that man can rebel against this love and alienate himself from the scheme of things. It was in this way that Boethius lost his way by means of a perverse love, but there is a hint of a promise that by love he will be brought back again to his true home.

Book III poem 9 continues the theme of God's government and control of the universe, which now finds its fullest treatment here in Book IV poem 6. The poem begins, like the first two of the group, with the description of the eternal peace of the heavens brought about by love. Echoing Book III poem 9 and the *Timaeus*, Philosophy moves on to the concord of the elements, of the seasons, and of birth and death, which includes mankind, and associates human affairs with the cosmic power of love. This leads her on to the author of this love, who stabilizes the universe by means of the triple movement of the Neoplatonists, away from God, turning, and coming back to Him.

In his emphasis on peace and on love, Boethius' commentators have seen a turning away from purely philosophical expression to something more akin to the writing of Christian authors like Pseudo-Dionysius and St Augustine. 'These poems have a temper and colouring that harmonises with the Christianity of their author.'[38] Whether this is so, or whether this is only the philosophical expression of an idea which goes

38. H. R. Patch on *Cons.* IV poem 6 in *Speculum* VIII, 1933, pp. 41–51: see also Klingner, op. cit., pp. 89–91.

to the Love of Empedocles,[39] these metres were certainly influential in later times; here are seeds of the thought of Dante (e.g. Beatrice's speech at the end of *Paradise* I) and the source of Chaucer's noble philosophy of love in *Troilus and Criseyde* (e.g. III, 1744 ff.).

The final poem of Book IV is a hymn of encouragement; the heroes Agamemnon, Odysseus and Hercules are celebrated as examples of achievement and as incentives on the final stage in the ascent to divinity. The discussion of Fate and Providence leads automatically into the Fifth Book. In the first chapter in answer to Boethius' inquiry the rule of the chain of causes is asserted and the existence of chance denied. The doctrine of Fate and Providence and of auxiliary causes stems from Plato, but here it is the Aristotelian development of the analysis of contingency into absolute and incidental cause and an Aristotelian example which Philosophy uses.[40] In the second chapter freedom is asserted in terms of the Platonic tradition— the more one shares in the divine, the more one achieves freedom. But the assertion that the choice of the individual soul is already known to Providence raises a further difficulty for Boethius – the apparent incompatibility between divine foreknowledge and freedom of the will. It is impossible to believe that God's Providence is fallible or dependent on temporal events; and yet foreknowledge, if it is to be truly knowledge, seems to impose a necessity upon events and actions which makes something monstrous of reward and punishment by God. There was little comfort for Boethius in the Augustinian solution which made human freewill dependent on the will of God, and he could find no satisfaction in any consolatory belief in predestination. And so he presses the argument forward until he can justify a belief in a human freedom sufficient to make room for moral responsibility.

His solution is provided by the combination of two considerations. First, the argument that the quality of knowledge

---

39. See Copleston, op. cit., I, ch. 8.   40. See note on p. 166.

depends on the capacity of the knower to know, not on the capacity of the object to be known; and second, the comparison of God's capacity to know with man's. This leads to Boethius' classic definition of eternity at the beginning of the last chapter of all. Its ultimate source, once again, though transmuted through the words of Proclus,[41] is in the *Timaeus* (37D E) and Plato's idea of time as a moving image of eternity. But Boethius' development is expressed with such lucidity and compactness that – like a number of his other definitions – it was accepted as authoritative by St Thomas Aquinas and the medieval schoolmen. Eternity is explained not in terms of quantity of life, but in terms of quality of life: in virtue of His complete, simultaneous and perfect possession of everlasting life, God, in Whom there is no past or future, but only timeless present, is eternal, while the world which only attains an endless series of moments, each lost as soon as it is attained, is merely perpetual. Boethius is pressing at the limits of what language can do.

This definition, the theory of knowledge, and the Aristotelian theory of the two kinds of necessity, form the core of Boethius' explanation of the compatibility of God's infallible knowledge and man's freedom of will. God is like a spectator at a chariot race; he watches the actions the charioteers perform, but this does not cause them. Similarly, God's vision of events which is eternal in the sense that God is eternal, means that He is a kind of spectator of all things simultaneously, past and future in one timeless present, without causing them. God is thus able to have knowledge of that which seen from the point of view of men in time is of uncertain occurrence.

This solution, of course, is meant as an answer to a particular kind of objection, and Boethius cannot be held to blame for not answering the kind of difficulty which might be raised today. Few have grappled more honestly with the problems

41. Cf. Barrett, op. cit., pp. 106–7 and 125–131.

of good and evil, fate and freewill; and if Boethius' answers are not entirely satisfactory, Philosophy's own words may remind us that 'it is not allowed to man to comprehend in thought all the ways of the divine work.'[42] This is the traditional attitude of Christianity since St Paul to those mysterious paradoxes of its doctrine which seem beyond human explanation, and in his firm insistence on the two opposing principles of human freedom and divine omniscience Boethius maintains a position perfectly in accord with Christian belief. By a stroke of calculated art we are left at the end with Philosophy's final exhortation, on a high plane, our gaze directed upwards, oblivious of the prison house.

IV. The Christianity of Boethius

And so we return to a question already proposed: what is the quality of Boethius' Christianity? It would not be difficult to show that in spite of his dependence on doctrines borrowed from Stoicism, from Plato and Aristotle and from Neo-platonism, there is little in the *Consolation* that is openly contrary to the tenets of Christianity. That which there is – the doctrine of *anamnesis* which presupposes the prior existence of the soul before birth, and the doctrine of the perpetuity of the world and the implicit denial of creation *ex nihilo* in the *Timaeus* poem[43] – is not of fundamental significance in the *Consolation*. Indeed there are important differences between Boethius and the Neoplatonism to which so much of his thought conforms. The Deity of Plotinus was absolutely transcendent and ineffable: from it through a hierarchy of powers such as Mind, World-Soul, Nature, etc., emanated the multiplicity of finite things. Plotinus' Neoplatonic successors actually increased the intermediary beings between God and

42. *Cons.*, IV, 6.

43. It is clear from his tractate *On the Catholic Faith* that Boethius believed the Christian doctrine of creation.

corporeal objects in order to emphasize the transcendence of the supreme Godhead, until they had constructed an 'amazing metaphysical museum, with all the entities and super-entities neatly labelled and arranged on their proper shelves'.[44]

All this, however, is quite alien to Boethius. He talks not of a supreme essence but of God: and he does not fill the gap between God and His world by any elaborate series of 'graded abstractions'.[45] Boethius' God is a personal God, a God to whom one can and should pray, as he reminds us in the closing words of the Consolation.

It is tempting, therefore, to argue that the reason why there is no mention of Christ and Christianity and no explicit reference to the Bible in the Consolation is that Boethius was writing a philosophical consolation, and not a theological one. 'Did you not read my title?' C. S. Lewis suggests Boethius would say:[46] 'I wrote philosophically, not religiously, because I had chosen the consolations of philosophy not those of religion as my subject. You might as well ask why a book on arithmetic does not use geometrical methods.'

It is true that an author would be expected to distinguish between disciplines and avoid introducing alien methods: thus when Boethius commends Philosophy for the way in which she has presented her arguments – in her own words they are 'arguments not sought from without but within the bounds of the matter we have been discussing'[47] – he appears to be commending her for sticking to the methods of philosophy and not importing anything from revelation. Here as in the rest of Boethius' work, we seem to meet a clear distinction between faith and reason.[48]

44. A. H. Armstrong, An Introduction to Ancient Philosophy, London (University Paperbacks), 1965, p. 201. Cf. Copleston, op. cit., I, ch. 45 and 46.

45. Rand, op. cit., p. 176.   46. The Discarded Image, p. 78.   47. III, 12.

48. Cf. above p. 13 and The Discarded Image, pp. 78–9; it should be noted that in IV, 4 Philosophy does not necessarily draw near the doctrines of Hell and Purgatory, since there was a place for punishment after death in the system of Plato: cf. Copleston, op. cit. I, ch. 21.

It seems strange, nevertheless, that writing in the presence of death Boethius still prefers reason to faith, and makes no mention of what must be the only fully meaningful consolation for a Christian, the Incarnation of Christ and the doctrine of grace.[49] For St Augustine, since man could accomplish nothing of himself, his absolute dependence on the grace of God was at the same time his freedom and happiness. But the Boethian doctrine of salvation, the ascent of the unaided individual by means of philosophical introspection and meditation to the knowledge of God, for all the closeness between Neoplatonic philosophy and post-Augustinian Christianity, is essentially pagan, in inspiration. This is the reason why in his *Dialogue of Cumfort* Sir Thomas More rejects the philosophers of old:[50] and it is interesting to note that even in the Middle Ages which accepted Boethius as a saint, commentators and scholars like Bruno of Corvey and John of Salisbury noticed the absence of Christian doctrine from the *Consolation*. It is hard to avoid the conclusion that Boethius professed a sort of *christianisme neutralisé*.[51] 'Boethius needs neither word nor Spirit nor mercy, neither church nor fellow-Christians in order to be what he is. It is therefore no accident but entirely appropriate that his last confession does not speak about Christ.'[52] He belonged to an age in which the ancient classical culture had become assimilated to Christianity, but not absorbed by it. The schools, for instance, were still pagan. And Boethius had not undergone the inner conversion of a Sidonius or an Ennodius: the ancient learning still preserved its hold upon him unimpaired.[53]

49. With the attitude of Boethius we might contrast that of Jean Gerson (1363–1429), Chancellor of the University of Paris, who in his *On the Consolation of Theology* rejects the consolations of philosophy because theology is superior to philosophy as grace is to nature, or mistress to handmaid. See H. R. Patch, *The Tradition of Boethius*, p. 108.

50. *A Dialogue of Cumfort against Tribulation*, Antverpiae, apud Johannem Foulerum, 1573, pp. 6–7.

51. M. Cappuyns, loc. cit., col. 360.   52. Campenhausen, op. cit., p. 312.

53. Cf. Helen Waddell, op. cit., ch. 1, *The Break with the Pagan Tradition*.

It may be, however, that the question of Boethius' Christianity has not been correctly formulated. It may be that if more were known of the intellectual climate of Roman society at the time the problem would appear in a different light.

The explanation may well lie, David Knowles suggests,[54]

in the changed attitude towards philosophy since the later middle ages. Between the days of Augustine and those of Siger of Brabant it was the universal conviction among those who thought seriously that there was a single true rational account of man and the universe and of an omnipotent and provident God, as valid in its degree as the revealed truths of Christianity. The great men of old, pagan though they might have been, had attained and expressed this truth in their philosophy could one but reproduce their teaching faithfully, and with their aid a true and sufficient answer could be given to the problems of human life and destiny. It was with these answers that the philosophical mind could meet the world and all the disasters of life. Behind the rational arguments, no doubt, in the unseen realm of the soul, an individual could meet the personal love and grace of Christ.[55]

v. The Text

In making this translation I have used Weinberger's text of the *Consolation* in the *Corpus Scriptorum Ecclesiasticorum*

54. *The Evolution of Medieval Thought*, Longmans, 1962, p. 55.

55. This valuable and important comment receives support from a number of passages where we perhaps get a glimpse of 'the unseen realm of the soul'. We have already noticed an echo of the Our Father (p. 25), and on p. 98 the possible influence of the Christian hymns is discussed. There is the passage mentioned above (p. 29) in which the parallel discipline of faith is implied, and there is the possible reference to Hell and Purgatory the existence of which Philosophy says she does not wish to discuss at that point (IV, 4). There are apparently some twenty-five places where without actually referring to the Bible, Boethius appears to echo Scriptural passages, cf. the *Index locorum Sacrae Scripturae* in Bieler's edition. In Book III, poem 12, if the commentators are right, Boethius tells Philosophy of the delight it causes him to hear her quoting the words of scripture: see note p. 112. Cf. also F. P. Pickering, *Notes on Fate and Fortune*, in *Mediaeval German Studies Presented to Frederick Norman*, London, 1965, pp. 1-15.

Latinorum, LXVII, Vienna/Leipzig, 1934, and also the edition of L. Bieler in the *Corpus Christianorum, Series Latina* XCIV, Turnhout, 1957. I have occasionally consulted the Loeb Classical Library edition of the *Theological Tractates* and *Consolation* by H. F. Stewart and E. K. Rand (Harvard University Press, 1918) and the translation of W. V. Cooper, London, 1902.

Apart from the problems that face all translators, the *Consolation* presents a number of other difficulties; the variety of the metres (which I have not attempted to reflect in any systematic way); the occasional use of problematic technical terms; the intermittent personification of figures such as Fortune and Nature. Even our 'prince of poets', Chaucer, turned it only into prose which was sometimes awkward. I cannot hope to have had better success.

The chief debts of the Introduction will be clear from my footnotes. For many helpful suggestions I should like to thank the present Joint Editor of the Penguin Classics, Mrs Betty Radice, and my gratitude is also due to my wife, and to my parents-in-law, Mr and Mrs W. Curtis, for their hospitality during the times when most of this translation was completed.

Lasborough, Gloucestershire
15 August 1967

The Consolation of Philosophy

BOOK I

I

I who once composed with eager zest
Am driven by grief to shelter in sad songs;
All torn the Muses' cheeks who spell the words
For elegies that wet my face with tears.
No terror could discourage them at least
From coming with me on my way.
They were the glory of my happy youth
And still they comfort me in hapless age.
Old age came suddenly by suffering sped,
And grief then bade her government begin:
My hair untimely white upon my head,
And I a worn out bone-bag hung with flesh.
Death would be happy if it spared the glad
But heeded invocations from the wretch.
But now Death's ears are deaf to hopeless cries,
His hands refuse to close poor weeping eyes.
First fickle Fortune gave me wealth short-lived,
Then in a moment all but ruined me.
Since Fortune changed her trustless countenance,
Small welcome to the days prolonging life.
Foolish the friends who called me happy then
Whose fall shows how my foothold was unsure.

WHILE I was quietly thinking these thoughts over to myself
and giving vent to my sorrow with the help of my pen, I
became aware of a woman standing over me. She was of
awe-inspiring appearance, her eyes burning and keen beyond
the usual power of men. She was so full of years that I could
hardly think of her as of my own generation, and yet she
possessed a vivid colour and undiminished vigour. It was
difficult to be sure of her height, for sometimes she was of
average human size, while at other times she seemed to touch

the very sky with the top of her head, and when she lifted herself even higher, she pierced it and was lost to human sight. Her clothes were made of imperishable material, of the finest thread woven with the most delicate skill. (Later she told me that she had made them with her own hands.) Their colour, however, was obscured by a kind of film as of long neglect, like statues covered in dust. On the bottom hem could be read the embroidered Greek letter Pi, and on the top hem the Greek letter Theta.[1] Between the two a ladder of steps rose from the lower to the higher letter. Her dress had been torn by the hands of marauders who had each carried off such pieces as he could get. There were some books in her right hand, and in her left hand she held a sceptre.

At the sight of the Muses of Poetry at my bedside dictating words to accompany my tears, she became angry.

'Who,' she demanded, her piercing eyes alight with fire, 'has allowed these hysterical sluts to approach this sick man's bedside? They have no medicine to ease his pains, only sweetened poisons to make them worse. These are the very women who kill the rich and fruitful harvest of Reason with the barren thorns of Passion. They habituate men to their sickness of mind instead of curing them. If as usual it was only some ordinary man you were carrying off a victim of your blandishments, it would matter little to me – there would be no harm done to my work. But this man has been nourished on the philosophies of Zeno and Plato. Sirens is a better name for you and your deadly enticements: be gone, and leave him for my own Muses to heal and cure.'

These rebukes brought blushes of shame into the Muses' cheeks, and with downcast eyes they departed in a dismal

1. In the first commentary on Porphyry's *Isagoge* or *Introduction to the Categories of Aristotle* Boethius says there are two kinds of philosophy, practical and speculative or contemplative, the Greek names for which begin with the letters Pi and Theta respectively. The former would seem to include moral philosophy and ethics, the latter theology, metaphysics and natural science or physics. *In Porph. Dial. I*, Migne, LXIV, 11a.

company. Tears had partly blinded me, and I could not make out who this woman of such imperious authority was. I could only fix my eyes on the ground overcome with surprise and wait in silence for what she would do next. She came closer and sat down on the edge of my bed. I felt her eyes resting on my face, downcast and lined with grief. Then sadly she began to recite the following lines about my confusion of mind.

II

'So sinks the mind in deep despair
And sight grows dim; when storms of life
Blow surging up the weight of care,
It banishes its inward light
And turns in trust to the dark without.
This was the man who once was free
To climb the sky with zeal devout
To contemplate the crimson sun,
The frozen fairness of the moon –
Astronomer once used in joy
To comprehend and to commune
With planets on their wandering ways.
This man, this man sought out the source
Of storms that roar and rouse the seas;
The spirit that rotates the world,
The cause that translocates the sun
From shining East to watery West;
He sought the reason why spring hours
Are mild with flowers manifest,
And who enriched with swelling grapes
Ripe autumn at the full of year.
Now see that mind that searched and made
All Nature's hidden secrets clear
Lie prostrate prisoner of night.
His neck bends low in shackles thrust,
And he is forced beneath the weight
To contemplate – the lowly dust.

'But it is time for healing, not lamenting,' she went on. Then, fixing her eyes intently upon me, she said, 'You are the man, are you not, who was brought up on the milk of my learning and fed on my own food until you reached maturity? I gave you arms to protect you and keep your strength unimpaired, but you threw them away. Surely you recognize me? And yet you do not speak. Is it shame or is it astonishment that keeps you silent? I should prefer it to be shame, but I see that it is not.'

When she saw that it was not that I would not speak, but that, dumbstruck, I could not, she gently laid her hand on my breast and said, 'It is nothing serious, only a touch of amnesia that he is suffering, the common disease of deluded minds. He has forgotten for a while who he is, but he will soon remember once he has recognized me. To make it easier for him I will wipe a little of the blinding cloud of worldly concern from his eyes.'

As she spoke she gathered her dress into a fold and wiped from my eyes the tears that filled them.

III

The night was put to flight, the darkness fled,
And to my eyes their former strength returned:
Like when the wild west wind accumulates
Black clouds and stormy darkness fills the sky:
The sun lies hid before the hour the stars
Should shine, and night envelops all the earth:
But should the North wind forth from his Thracian cave
Lash at the darkness and loose the prisoner day,
Out shines the sun with sudden light suffused
And dazzles with its rays the blinking eye.

In the same way the clouds of my grief dissolved and I drank in the light. With my thoughts recollected I turned to examine the face of my physician. I turned my eyes and fixed my gaze upon her, and I saw that it was my nurse in whose house I had been cared for since my youth – Philosophy. I asked her why she had come down from the heights of heaven to my lonely place of banishment.

'Is it to suffer false accusation along with me?' I asked.

'Why, my child,' she replied, 'should I desert you? Why should I not share your labour and the burden you have been saddled with because of the hatred of my name? Should I be frightened by being accused? Or cower in fear as if it were something unprecedented? This is hardly the first time wisdom has been threatened with danger by the forces of evil. In olden times, too, before the time of my servant Plato, I fought many a great battle against the reckless forces of folly. And then, in Plato's own lifetime, his master Socrates was unjustly put to death – a victorious death won with me at his side. After that the mobs of Epicureans and Stoics and the others each did all they could to seize for themselves the inheritance of wisdom that he left. As part of their plunder they tried to carry me off, but I fought and struggled, and in the fight the robe was torn which I had woven with my own hands. They tore off little pieces from it and went away in the fond belief that they had obtained the whole of philosophy. The sight of traces of my clothing on them gained them the reputation among the ignorant of being my familiars, and as a result many of them became corrupted by the ignorance of the uninitiated mob.

'But even if you do not know the stories of the foreign philosophers, how Anaxagoras was banished from Athens, how Socrates was put to death by poisoning, and how Zeno was tortured, you do know of Romans like Canius, Seneca and Soranus, whose memory is still fresh and celebrated. The sole cause of their tragic sufferings was their obvious, and complete contempt of the pursuits of immoral men which my teaching had instilled in them. It is hardly surprising if we are driven by the blasts of storms when our chief aim on this sea of life is to displease wicked men. And though their numbers are great, we can afford to despise them because they

persecu-
tion for
devotion
to Phil.

have no one to lead them and are carried along only by ignorance which distracts them at random first one way then another. When their forces attack us in superior numbers, our general conducts a tactical withdrawal of his forces to a strong point, and they are left to encumber themselves with useless plunder. Safe from their furious activity on our ramparts above, we can smile at their efforts to collect all the most useless booty: our citadel cannot fall to the assaults of folly.'

IV

'Let men compose themselves and live at peace,
    Set haughty fate beneath their feet,
And look unmoved on fortune good and bad,
    And keep unchanging countenance:
Unmoved they'll stand before the ocean's rage
    Which churns up waves from deep below,
Unmoved by restless Mount Vesuvius,
    Her furnace burst and hurling flames,
Unmoved by fiery thunderbolts in flight
    Which sweep in ruin towers on high.
Why then are miserable men in awe
    When tyrants rage impotently?
If first you rid yourself of hope and fear
    You have disarmed the tyrant's wrath:
But whosoever quakes in fear or hope,
    Drifting and losing mastery,
Has cast away his shield, has left his place,
And binds the chain with which he will be bound.

'Do you understand this,' she went on, 'and have my words penetrated your mind? – or are you like the proverbial donkey, deaf to the lyre? Tell me why you are weeping and why your eyes are full of tears. As Homer says,[2]

    Speak out and hide it not within.

If you want the doctor's help, you must reveal the wound.'
    I collected my thoughts and replied with vigour, 'Surely

2. *Iliad*, I, 363.

the severity of Fortune's attack on me needs no further mention; it is self evident. Look at the mere appearance of this place. Is it the library of my house which you chose yourself as a place of sure repose and where you so often used to sit with me discussing all the topics of philosophy?[3] Are my clothes the same and my face the same as when I used to probe the secrets of nature with you, and you used to describe the various paths of the planets with your stick and relate human ethics and the whole of human life to the patterns of the celestial order?

'This, then, is how you reward your followers. And yet it was no one but you who commended Plato's opinion that commonwealths would be blessed if they should be ruled by philosophers or if their rulers should happen to have studied philosophy.[4] You took your cue from him and said that the reason why it was necessary for philosophers to take part in government was to prevent the reins of government falling into the hands of wicked and unprincipled men to the ruin and destruction of the good. And it was upon this authority that I decided to transfer to public administration what I had learned from you in the course of our private leisure. You and God, who has sowed you in the minds of wise men, are my witnesses that the only consideration to impel me to any office was a general desire for good. This was the reason why I had no alternative but grimly to resist evil and why in the struggle to defend justice I have always been indifferent to the hatred I inspired in men who wielded greater power than mine – an indifference inspired by the knowledge that I had freely followed my conscience. I have countless times opposed the attacks of Cunigast on the fortunes of some defenceless person, or stopped Triguilla, the Prefect of the Palace, from

3. Boethius speaks specifically of 'matters human and divine' by which he means the two traditional divisions of philosophy into morals and natural science. See note p. 36.

4. See Plato's *Republic*, 473d. Penguin Classics version, p. 233.

some injustice he had begun or already carried through. And I have countless times interposed my authority to protect wretched men from danger when they were hounded by the endless false accusations of the barbarians in their continuous and unpunished lust for wealth. I have never been moved from justice to injustice by anything. I have ached with as much pain as the provinces themselves to see their fortunes ruined by private plundering and public taxation. When the terrible famine came and a ruinous and inexplicable measure of forced sale of food supplies was announced which seemed calculated to crush the province of Campania with poverty, I took up the cudgels against the Pretorian Prefect in the interest of the common good, and although the king knew of my actions, I succeeded in the struggle to block the sale.

'Again, in their hope and ambition the palace jackals had already swallowed up the wealth of an ex-consul called Paulinus, when I snatched him from their very jaws. Another ex-consul, Albinus, had been presumed guilty and I had to set myself against the hatred of the Public Prosecutor,[5] Cyprian, to save him from punishment. You must surely agree that the opposition I provoked against me was considerable. But I ought to have been the safer among the rest, as my love of justice led me to keep no reserve of favour among the courtiers for my greater safety. Yet who were the informers who struck me down? One was Basilius. He had previously been dismissed from the royal service and was forced into impeaching me by his debts. Two others were Opilio and Gaudentius. A royal decree had sentenced them to banishment because of their countless frauds, and to avoid complying they had protected themselves by seeking sanctuary. When the news

5. To translate the Latin title *referendarius* as I have done as 'Public Prosecutor' is perhaps true to Boethius' attitude to his accuser, but not strictly accurate. No one English word corresponds to the Latin: the *referendarius* was 'an officer whose duty it was to prepare cases that were to come before the King's Consistorium and to make a clear and impartial statement of the cases in the presence of the court' (Helen M. Barrett, *Boethius*, p. 52).

reached the king he made a proclamation that unless they had left the city of Ravenna by the appointed day they would be driven out with their foreheads branded. There could scarcely be greater severity than that. Yet the very same day they laid information against me and the denunciation was accepted. Surely my actions didn't deserve that? And surely the fact that my conviction was prejudged didn't make just men of my accusers? Fortune should have blushed at the sight of innocence accused, or at least at the depravity of my accusers.

'But you want to know the <u>nub of the charge</u> against me. <u>I am accused of having desired the safety of the</u> Senate. And as for the manner, I am accused of having prevented an informer from delivering certain papers with which he intended to show the Senate guilty of treason. My Lady, tell me what your advice is: am I to deny the charge to avoid causing you shame? But the fact is that I did desire the safety of the Senate and will never cease to. Perhaps I should confess, except that my attempt to prevent the informer was not continued. Should I count it a crime to have desired the safety of the Senate? They at any rate by their own decrees about me have made it a crime. Imprudence may deceive itself, but it cannot alter the true value of things, and the ruling of Socrates that it is quite wrong to assent to falsehood and conceal truth forbids me either to hide truth or be party to untruth.[6] But I leave it to you and to the wise to judge of these events which I have committed to writing to ensure that they are remembered, and to preserve for posterity the true sequence of events.[7]

'As for the forged letters cited as evidence that I had hoped for the freedom of Rome, there is little purpose in speaking of them. It would have been obvious that they were forgeries

6. Boethius is thinking either of Plato's *Theaetetus*, 151 d or the *Republic*, 485c, Penguin Classics translation, p. 245.
7. Unfortunately this account, if it was ever completed, is now lost.

had I been allowed to make use of what carries the greatest weight in all such matters – the confession of the very informers.

'But there is no freedom left to hope for. If only there were, I would have replied with the same retort as Canius made to the Emperor Caligula when he was accused of being involved in a plot against him. "If *I* had known of it," he said, "*you* would not."

'Grief has not so dulled my wits in all this as to make me complain that the wicked have piled up their crimes against virtue; but what does fill me with wonder is that they have brought their hopes to fruition. It may be part of human weakness to have evil wishes, but it is nothing short of monstrous that God should look on while every criminal is allowed to achieve his purpose against the innocent. If this is so, it was hardly without reason that one of your household[8] asked where evil comes from if there is a god, and where good comes from if there isn't.

'Even supposing there may have been some justice in that the evil men who are out for the blood of all good men and of all the Senate also sought my own death when they saw me championing them, surely I did not deserve the same treatment from the members of the Senate themselves? You remember, I am sure, since you were always present to give me your guidance when I was preparing a speech or some course of action – you remember how at Verona a charge of treason was made against Albinus and how in his eagerness to see the total destruction of the Senate the king tried to extend the charge to them all in spite of their universal innocence; and you remember how I defended them with complete indifference to any danger, and you know that I am telling the truth and have never boasted of any merit of mine. For as often as a

8. The philosopher in question appears to have been Epicurus (fr. 374 quoted by Lactantius, *De Ira Dei* 13, 21, *Opera Omnia* II i, ed. S. Brandt and G. Laubman, *Corpus Scriptorum Ecclesiasticorum Latinorum*, Vienna, 1893).

man receives the reward of fame for his boasting, the conscience that indulges in self congratulation loses something of its secret merit.

'And now you see the outcome of my innocence – instead of reward for true goodness, punishment for a crime I did not commit. Yet no confession however clear-cut of any crime has ever found a jury so united in their agreement on the severest penalty that some were not softened either by the thought of human weakness or the universal uncertainty of human fortune. If I had been charged with planning to burn down churches, or plotting the sacrilegious murder of priests, or aiming to massacre all men of worth, I would still have been brought into court and either have confessed or been convicted before the sentence was carried out. But here I am, nearly five hundred miles away, condemned to death and to have my property confiscated, silenced, and with no opportunity to offer a defence, all because of a somewhat too willing support of the Senate. How they deserve that no one should ever be convicted on a similar charge!

'Even those who laid the information against me could see the dignity the charge conferred, and in order to obscure it by the addition of some other charge, they lyingly alleged that in my ambition for high office I had stained my conscience with acts of sacrilege. But you had taken up your dwelling within me and used to drive from my mind every thought of human advancement and there could be no place for sacrilege beneath your gaze. You used daily to instill in my ears and thoughts that Pythagorean maxim, "Follow God". And since you were there lifting me up to such a pitch of excellence as to make me like a god, it was scarcely fitting that I should angle for the help of the vilest of spirits. Then there is the blameless life in my home, my friendship with the most honourable of men, and the sanctity of Symmachus, my father-in-law, a man worthy of the same veneration as yourself; all these guarantee me against suspicion of this charge. But the wickedness of it is that it is from you yourself that they obtain their trust in this great accusation. For the very fact that I am steeped in your teaching and trained in your morality seems to them to prove that I have been engaged in evil practice. It is not enough that my devotion to you has not helped me at all, but you are now made the victim of the hatred that should be directed at me alone. Over and above all this, another weight is added to my load of ills in that the world does not judge actions on their merit, but on their chance results, and they consider that only those things which are blessed with a happy outcome have been undertaken with sound advice. It is always the unfortunate who are first to be deserted by the goodwill of men.

'I have no mind to recall all the rumours that are circulating and the discord of their multifarious opinions. I will just say that the final burden which adversity heaps on her victims, is that when some accusation is made against them, they are believed to have deserved all that they suffer. And so, stripped of every possession, thrust from my offices, and with my reputation in ruins, for doing a favour I have received a punishment. I seem to see the wicked haunts of criminals overflowing with happiness and joy; I seem to see all the most desperate of men threatening new false denunciations; I seem to see good men lying prostrate with fear at the danger I am in while all abandoned villains are encouraged to attempt every crime in the expectation of impunity or even in the hope of reward for its accomplishment; and I seem to see the innocent deprived of peace and safety and even of all chance of self defence.'

V

'Creator of the starry heavens,
Lord on thy everlasting throne,
Thy power turns the moving sky
And makes the stars obey fixed laws.

Thou makest lesser stars grow dim
Before the Moon's reflected rays
When opposite her kinsman bright:
Then closer to the Sun she moves
And loses all her borrowed light.
Thou the Evening Star dost make
Rise cold and clear in early night,
And change, as Morning Star, his reins
To pale before the new sun's light.
When Winter's cold has stripped the trees
Thou holdest day in confines tight:
When Summer comes with torrid heat
Thou givest swifter hours to night.
Thy power rules the changing year:
The tender leaves the North wind stole
The Spring West wind makes reappear;
The seeds that Winter saw new sown
The Summer burns as crops full-grown.
All things obey their ancient law
And all perform their proper tasks;
All things thou holdest in strict bounds, –
To human acts alone denied
Thy fit control as Lord of all.
Why else does slippery Fortune change
So much, and punishment more fit
For crime oppress the innocent?
Corrupted men sit throned on high;
By strange reversal evilness
Downtreads the necks of holy men.
Bright virtue lies in dark eclipse
By clouds obscured, and unjust men
Heap condemnation on the just;
No punishment for perjury
Or lies adorned with speciousness.
They use their power when whimsy bids,
And love to subjugate great kings
Whose sway holds countless men in fear.
O Thou who bindest bonds of things

Look down on all earth's wretchedness;
Of this great work is man so mean
A part, by Fortune to be tossed?
Lord, hold the rushing waves in check,
And with the bond thou rul'st the stars,
Make stable all the lands of earth.'

Throughout this long and noisy display of grief, Philosophy remained unperturbed. When I had finished she looked at me calmly and said:

'The moment I saw your sad and tear-stained looks, they told me that you had been reduced to the misery of banishment; but unless you had told me, I would still not have known how far you had been banished. However, it is not simply a case of your having been banished far from your home; you have wandered away yourself, or if you prefer to be thought of as having been banished, it is you yourself that have been the instrument of it. No one else could ever have done it. For if you remember the country you came from, it is not governed by majority rule like Athens of old, but, if I may quote Homer, [9]

One is its lord and one its king;

and rather than having them banished, He prefers to have a large body of subjects. Submitting to His governance and obeying His laws is freedom. You seem to have forgotten the oldest law of your community, that any man who has chosen to make his dwelling there has the sacred right never to be banished. So there can be no fear of exile for any man within its walls and moat. On the other hand, if anyone stops wanting to live there, he automatically stops deserving it.

'And so it is not the sight of this place which gives me concern but your own appearance, and it is not the walls of your library with their glass and ivory decoration that I am looking for, but the seat of your mind. That is the place where

9. *Iliad*, 2, 204.

I once stored away – not my books, but – the thing that makes them have any value, the philosophy they contain.

'As for what you said about your services to the common good, it was but scant measure considering the great number of things you have done. Then your talk about the truth or untruth of the charges against you is only what is known to many. And you were right in thinking that the crimes and deceits of your accusers needed but cursory mention since they are the continual talk of the people who are more richly and better acquainted with their every detail. Then you spoke with considerable vehemence about the Senate's unjust behaviour and spoke with grief of my inclusion in the accusations and wept tears at the damage done to my injured reputation. And last of all, with your anger flaring up against Fortune, and the bitter complaint that reward is not measured out according to desert, in your final angry verses you prayed that the same peace that rules in the heavens should rule on earth.

'In your present state of mind, while this great tumult of emotion has fallen upon you and you are torn this way and that by alternating fits of grief, wrath and anguish, it is hardly time for the more powerful remedies. I will use gentler medicines. It is as if you had become swollen and calloused under the influence of these disturbing passions, and by their more gentle action they will temper you ready to receive the strength of a sharper medicament.'

VI

'If when summer solstice brings
   The Crab with parching heat,
In furrows that refuse the seed
   The farmer sows his wheat,
No crops will spring to glad his hopes
   And acorns he shall eat.
You would not search the woodside gay
   To pick a springtime flower

49

When all the shuddering country groans
　　Before the North Wind's power.
Nor would you seek with greedy hand
　　To pluck your vines in May;
The wine god gives his gift of grapes
　　When Autumn's on the way.
For God has fixed the seasons' tasks
　　And each receives its own:
No power is free to disarray
　　The order God has shown.
Should then some being precipitate
　　Aspire to quit its place,
The Lord would not allow success
　　Its mutiny to grace.

'Will you first then let me discover your state of mind and test it with a few simple questions? That way I can discover the best method of curing you.'

'Ask what you like,' I replied, 'and I will answer.'

'Do you believe that this life consists of haphazard and chance events, or do you think it is governed by some rational principle?'

'I could never believe that events of such regularity are due to the haphazards of chance. In fact I know that God the Creator watches over His creation. The day will never come that sees me abandon the truth of this belief.'

'It is true,' she said, 'and indeed it is the very thing you were singing of just now when you were deploring the fact that only mankind is outside God's care. It was your firm conviction that all other things were governed by reason. So how you can be sick when you hold so healthy a belief is quite beyond my understanding. However, let us carry our examination deeper. I feel there is something missing somewhere. Tell me, then, since you have no doubts that the world is governed by God, what are the means by which you think He guides it?'

'I can't answer the question,' I replied, 'because I don't understand what it means.'

'I was right, then,' she said, 'in thinking that something was missing. Your defences have been breached and your mind has been infiltrated by the fever of emotional distraction. So tell me, do you remember what is the end and purpose of things and the goal to which the whole of Nature is directed?'

'I did hear it once,' I said, 'but my memory has been blunted by grief.'

'Well, do you know the source from which all things come?'

'Yes,' I replied, and said that it was God.

'How can it be then, that you know the beginning of things but don't know their end? The peculiarity of these disturbances is that they have just enough power to move a man from his usual position, but can't quite throw him over and totally uproot him. I want you to answer this too: do you remember that you are a man?'

'Why shouldn't I?' I said.

'Can you, then, tell me what man is?'

'Are you asking me if I know whether man is a rational and mortal animal? I do know it and I acknowledge that that is what I am.'

'Are you sure you are not something more?'

'Quite sure.'

'Now I know the other cause, or rather the major cause of your illness: you have forgotten your true nature. And so I have found out in full the reason for your sickness and the way to approach the task of restoring you to health. It is because you are confused by loss of memory that you wept and claimed you had been banished and robbed of all your possessions. And it is because you don't know the end and purpose of things that you think the wicked and the criminal have power and happiness. And because you have forgotten the means by which the world is governed you believe these ups and downs of fortune happen haphazardly. These are grave causes and they lead not only to illness but even death. Thanks, however, to the Author of all health, nature has not quite abandoned you. In your true belief about the world's government – that it is subject to divine reason and not the haphazards of chance – there lies our greatest hope of rekindling your health. You need have no fears then, now that this tiny spark has blazed with the fire of life. Still, as it is not yet time for stronger medicine, and as it is the accepted opinion that the nature of the mind is such that for every true belief it rejects, it assumes a false one from which the fog of distraction rises to blot out its true insight, I will try to lessen this particular fog little by little by applying gentle remedies of only medium strength. In this way the darkness of the ever treacherous passions may be dispelled, and you will be able to see the resplendent light of truth.'

VII

'In dark clouds
Hidden
The stars can shed
No light.
If boisterous winds
Stir the sea
Causing a storm,
Waves once crystal
Like days serene
Soon turn opaque
And thick with mud
Prevent the eye
Piercing the water.
Streams that wander
From tall hills
Down descending
Often dash
Against a rock
Torn from the hillside.

BOOK I

If you desire
To look on truth
And follow the path
With unswerving course,
Rid yourself
Of joy and fear,
Put hope to flight,
And banish grief.
The mind is clouded
And bound in chains
Where these hold sway.'

BOOK II

I

AFTER this she fell silent for a while and the very forbearance of her silence made me turn my attention to her. At this she began to speak again.

'If I have fully diagnosed the cause and nature of your condition, you are wasting away in pining and longing for your former good fortune. It is the loss of this which, as your imagination works upon you, has so corrupted your mind. I know the many disguises of that monster, Fortune, and the extent to which she seduces with friendship the very people she is striving to cheat, until she overwhelms them with unbearable grief at the suddenness of her desertion. If you can recall to mind her character, her methods, and the kind of favour she proffers, you will see that in her you did not have and did not lose anything of value. But I am sure it will require no hard work on my part to bring all this back to your memory. It used to be your way whenever she came near with her flattery to attack her with manly arguments and hound her with pronouncements taken from the oracle of my shrine. However, no sudden change of circumstances ever occurs without some upheaval in the mind; and that is why you, too, have deserted for a while your usual calm.

'It is time, then, for you to take a little mild and pleasant nourishment which by being absorbed into your body will prepare the way for something stronger. Let us bring to bear the persuasive powers of sweet-tongued rhetoric, powers which soon go astray from the true path unless they follow my instructions. And let us have as well Music, the maid-servant of my house, to sing us melodies of varying mood.

'What is it then O mortal man, that has thrown you down into the slough of grief and despondency? You must have

seen something strange and unexpected. But you are wrong
if you think Fortune has changed towards you. Change is her
normal behaviour, her true nature. In the very act of changing
she has preserved her own particular kind of constancy towards
you. She was exactly the same when she was flattering you
and luring you on with enticements of a false kind of happiness.
You have discovered the changing faces of the random
goddess. To others she still veils herself, but to you she has
revealed herself to the full. If you are satisfied with her ways,
you must accept them and not complain. But if you shudder
to think of her unreliability, you must turn away and have
nothing more to do with her dangerous games. She has
caused you untold sorrow when she ought to have been a
source of peace. For she has left you, she in whose constancy
no man can ever trust. Do you really hold dear that kind of
happiness which is destined to pass away? Do you really value
the presence of Fortune when you cannot trust her to stay
and when her departure will plunge you in sorrow? And if it
is impossible to keep her at will and if her flight exposes men
to ruin, what else is such a fleeting thing except a warning of
coming disaster? It will never be sufficient just to notice what
is under one's nose: prudence calculates what the outcome of
things will be. Either way Fortune's very mutability deprives
her threats of their terror and her enticements of their allure.
And last of all, once you have bowed your neck beneath her
yoke, you ought to bear with equanimity whatever happens
on Fortune's playground. If after freely choosing her as the
mistress to rule your life you want to draw up a law to control
her coming and going, you will be acting without any
justification and your very impatience will only worsen a
lot which you cannot alter. Commit your boat to the winds
and you must sail whichever way they blow, not just where
you want. If you were a farmer who entrusts his seed to the
fields, you would balance the bad years against the good. So
now you have committed yourself to the rule of Fortune, you

must acquiesce in her ways. If you are trying to stop her wheel from turning,[1] you are of all men the most obtuse. For if it once begins to stop, it will no longer be the wheel of chance.

> 'With domineering hand she moves the turning wheel,
> Like currents in a treacherous bay swept to and fro:
> Her ruthless will has just deposed once fearful kings
> While trustless still, from low she lifts a conquered head;
> No cries of misery she hears, no tears she heeds,
> But steely hearted laughs at groans her deeds have wrung.
> Such is the game she plays, and so she tests her strength;
> Of mighty power she makes parade when one short hour
> Sees happiness from utter desolation grow.'

II

'I would like to continue our discussion a while by using Fortune's own arguments, and I would like you to consider whether her demands are just. "Why do you burden me each day, mortal man," she asks, "with your querulous accusations? What harm have I done you? What possessions of yours have I stolen? Choose any judge you like and sue me for possession of wealth and rank, and if you can show that any part of these belongs by right to any mortal man, I will willingly concede that what you are seeking to regain really did belong to you. When nature brought you forth from your mother's womb I

1. Though not original – the wheel of Fortune was a favourite expression of Cicero for instance – this is one of the most striking images in the *Consolation* and is the source of the many medieval allusions to Fortune and her wheel: cf. *Romance of the Rose*, 4807 ff.; Dante, *Hell*, VII, 61 ff.; Chaucer, *Troilus and Criseyde*, IV, 1 ff. There is a fine thirteenth-century painting of the Wheel of Fortune in the choir of Rochester Cathedral. Cf. A. B. Cook, *Zeus, Jupiter and the Oak*, *The Classical Review*, XVII, 1903, p. 421; D. M. Robinson, *The Wheel of Fortune*, *Classical Philology*, XLI, 1946, pp. 207 ff. For the Middle Ages: Italo Siciliano, *François Villon et les thèmes poétiques du moyen âge*, Paris, 1934, pp. 291 ff.; Emile Mâle, *The Gothic Image* translated by Dora Hussey, Fontana Library ed., pp. 94 ff.; H. R. Patch, *The Goddess Fortuna in Medieval Literature*, Cambridge, Mass., 1927.

received you naked and devoid of everything and fed you from my own resources. I was inclined to favour you, and I brought you up – and this is what makes you lose patience with me – with a measure of indulgence, surrounding you with all the splendour and affluence at my command. Now I have decided to withdraw my hand. You have been receiving a favour as one who has had the use of another's possessions, and you have no right to complain as if what you have lost was fully your own. You have no cause to begin groaning at me: I have done you no violence. Wealth, honours and the like are all under my jurisdiction. They are my servants and know their mistress. When I come, they come with me, and when I go, they leave as well. I can say with confidence that if the things whose loss you are bemoaning were really yours, you could never have lost them. Surely I am not the only one to be denied the exercise of my rights? The heavens are allowed to bring forth the bright daylight and lay it to rest in the darkness of night: the year is allowed alternately to deck the face of the earth with fruit and flowers and to disfigure it with cloud and cold. The sea is allowed either to be calm and inviting or to rage with storm-driven breakers. Shall man's insatiable greed bind me to a constancy which is alien to my ways? Inconstancy is my very essence; it is the game I never cease to play as I turn my wheel in its ever changing circle, filled with joy as I bring the top to the bottom and the bottom to the top. Yes, rise up on my wheel if you like, but don't count it an injury when by the same token you begin to fall, as the rules of the game will require. You must surely have been aware of my ways. You must have heard of Croesus, king of Lydia, who was once able to terrorize his enemy Cyrus, only to be reduced to misery and be condemned to be burnt alive: only a shower of rain saved him.[2] And you must have heard of Aemilius Paulus and how he wept tears of pity at all the disasters that had overwhelmed

2. Herodotus, I, 75 ff.

his prisoner, Perses, the last king of Macedonia.[3] Isn't this what tragedy commemorates with its tears and tumult – the overthrow of happy realms by the random strokes of Fortune? When you were a little boy you must have heard Homer's story of the two jars standing in God's house, the one full of evil and the other of good.[4] Now, you have had more than your share of the good, but have I completely deserted you? Indeed, my very mutability gives you just cause to hope for better things. So you should not wear yourself out by setting your heart on living according to a law of your own in a world that is shared by everyone.

' "If Plenty from her well-stocked horn
    With generous hand should distribute
As many gifts as grains of sand
The sea churns up when strong winds blow,
Or stars that shine on starlit nights,
The human race would still repeat
    Its querulous complaints.
Though God should gratify their prayers
With open-handed gifts of gold
And furbish greed with pride of rank,
All that God gave would seem as naught.
Rapacious greed soon swallows all
And opens other gaping mouths;
No reins will serve to hold in check
The headlong course of appetite
Once such largess has fanned the flames
    Of lust to have and hold:
No man is rich who shakes and groans
    Convinced that he needs more." '

III

'If Fortune herself had been speaking, she would have left you without a single syllable you could utter by way of reply. But if there is some argument which you can offer as a just

3. Livy, XLV, 7 ff.   4. *Iliad*, 24, 527 ff. Penguin translation, p. 451.

defence for your complaints, you must put it forward and we will give you a hearing.'

And so I had my turn.

'All that you have said,' I began, 'is certainly plausible and well sugared with the sweet honey of rhetoric and music. But it is only while one is actually listening that one is filled with pleasure, and for the wretched, the pain of their suffering goes deeper. So as soon as your words stop sounding in our ears, the mind is weighed down again by its deep seated melancholy.'

'It is true,' she rejoined, 'for none of this is meant to be a cure for your condition, but simply a kind of application to help soothe a grief still resistant to treatment. When the time comes, I will apply something calculated to penetrate deep inside. In the meantime stop thinking of yourself as plunged in misery. Have you forgotten how fortunate you have been in many ways? I will not dwell on it, but when you were orphaned you were taken up into the care of men of the highest rank and chosen to marry into families which boasted the state's most distinguished citizens. Even before you became their kinsman, you had begun to win their love, and that is the most precious kind of kinship of all. There was no one who would not have called you the luckiest man in the world, considering the glory reflected from your new connexions, the modesty of your wife, and the blessings your two sons proved to be. I have no desire to waste time on ordinary matters, so I will pass over the various dignities you received while still a young man, dignities which are denied the majority of men at any age. I want to come straight to the outstanding culmination of your fortune. If the enjoyment of any earthly blessing brings with it any measure of happiness, the memory of that splendid day can never be destroyed by the burden however great of growing evil. I mean the day that you saw your two sons amid the crowding senators and the rapture of the people carried forth from your house to be consuls together – the day they took their official seats in the senate chamber to listen to you delivering the speech of congratulation to the king and saw the genius of your oratory receive its crowning recognition: the same day as you sat in the stadium between the two consuls and as if it were a military triumph let your largess fulfil the wildest expectations of the people packed in their seats around you.

'In my opinion you beguiled Fortune with empty words so long as you had her caresses and she cherished you as her darling. And you went off with a gift never before bestowed on any private individual. Perhaps you would like to reckon up the score with her? You will find this is the very first time she has turned an unfriendly eye upon you. If you thought of all the things that have happened to you, what kind of things they were, and whether they were happy or unhappy things, you would not be able to say you have not been fortunate up to now. On the other hand, if you do not consider that you have been lucky because your onetime reasons for rejoicing have passed away, you cannot now think of yourself as in misery, because the very things that seem miserable are also passing away. Why behave like a stranger newly arrived on the stage of life? You know there is no constancy in human affairs, when a single swift hour can often bring a man to nothing. For even if you can't expect any permanence in a life of chance events, on the last day of one's life there is a kind of death for Fortune even when she stays with one. What do you think the answer is – does a man desert Fortune when he dies, or does she desert him by running away?

> 'When Phoebus in his ruby car
> Through heaven begins to spread his light,
> Thereupon each pale-faced star
> Grows dim before his radiance bright.
> The woodlands at the breath of spring
> Carmine coloured roses wear,
> But let the wind his cold blasts fling,

They'll leave the thorns of beauty bare.
Often the sea lies calm and still,
Its shimmering waves at rest,
And often the north wind churns the deep
With raging storms and mad unrest.
The world stays rarely long the same,
So great its instability,
So put your faith in transient luck,
And trust in wealth's mortality!
 In law eternal it lies decreed
 That naught from change is ever freed.'

IV

'All that you say is true,' I agreed. 'You truly are mother of all virtues, and I cannot deny the speed with which I rose to prosperity. It is the very thing, in fact, which makes me burn with grief as I remember it. In all adversity of fortune, the most wretched kind is once to have been happy.'[5]

'But you are suffering because of your misguided belief, and you can't blame events for that,' she replied. 'If you are really so moved by the empty name of chance happiness, you can reckon up with me now the number of the very great blessings you still enjoy. And if you find that you still possess that which among all the gifts of Fortune was most precious to you and find it through God's power unharmed and still untouched, you will hardly be able to talk about misfortune with any justice while you still possess outstanding blessings.

'Take your father-in-law, Symmachus, one of the most precious ornaments of the human race; he is still full of vigour and – something you would willingly pay for with your life – a man wholly composed of wisdom and virtue, who disregards his own sufferings and weeps for yours. Your wife, too, is alive, a lady unsurpassed in nobility and modesty

5. This famous saying, like others in the *Consolation*, is echoed by later writers: cf. Dante, *Hell*, V, 121 ff.

of character; to sum up all her qualities in a word, I would say she is the mirror of her father. She is, as I say, still alive and in her disgust with this life draws every breath for you alone. She longs for you and is consumed with tears and suffering, one thing in which I would concede that your happiness is diminished. I don't know what more to add about your consular sons. Now, as when they were boys, they reflect the example of their father's and grandfather's character. You are a happy man, then, if you know where your true happiness lies, since when the chief concern of mortal men is to keep their hold on life, you even now possess blessings which no one can doubt are more precious than life itself. So dry your tears. Fortune has not yet turned her hatred against all your blessings. The storm has not yet broken upon you with too much violence. Your anchors are holding firm and they permit you both comfort in the present, and hope in the future.'

'And I pray that they will hold,' I said. 'So long as they do, we will ride the storm out. But look how far events have gone since the time of my glory.'

'If you are no longer dissatisfied with the whole of your fortune, we have made a little progress,' she said. 'But I can't put up with your dilly-dallying and the dramatization of your care-worn grief-stricken complaints that something is lacking from your happiness. No man is so completely happy that something somewhere does not clash with his condition. It is the nature of human affairs to be fraught with anxiety; they never prosper perfectly and they never remain constant. In one man's case you will find riches offset by the shame of a humble birth and in another's noble birth offset by publicity unwelcome on account of the crippling poverty of his family fortunes. Some men are blessed with both wealth and noble birth, but are unhappy because they have no wife. Some are happily married but without children, and husband their money for an heir of alien blood. Some again have been blessed with children only to weep over their misdeeds. No one finds it easy to accept the lot Fortune has sent him. There is something in the case of each of us that escapes the notice of the man who has not experienced it, but causes horror to the man who has. Remember, too, that all the most happy men are over-sensitive. They have never experienced adversity and so unless everything obeys their slightest whim they are prostrated by every minor upset, so trifling are the things that can detract from the complete happiness of a man at the summit of fortune. How many men do you think would believe themselves almost in heaven if they possessed even the smallest part of the luck you still enjoy? This very place which is banishment to you is home to those who live here. So nothing is miserable except when you think it so, and vice versa, all luck is good luck to the man who bears it with equanimity. No one is so happy that he would not want to change his lot if he gives in to impatience. Such is the bittersweetness of human happiness. To him that enjoys it, it may seem full of delight, but he cannot prevent it slipping away when it will. It is evident, therefore, how miserable the happiness of human life is; it does not remain long with those who are patient, and doesn't satisfy those who are troubled.

'Why then do you mortal men seek after happiness outside yourselves, when it lies within you? You are led astray by error and ignorance. I will briefly show you what complete happiness hinges upon. If I ask you whether there is anything more precious to you than your own self, you will say no. So if you are in possession of yourself you will possess something you would never wish to lose and something Fortune could never take away. In order to see that happiness can't consist in things governed by chance, look at it this way. If happiness is the highest good of rational nature and anything that can be taken away is not the highest good – since it is surpassed by what can't be taken away – Fortune by her very mutability can't hope to lead to happiness.

'Again, the man who is borne along by happiness which can at any time fail, either knows or does not know its unreliability. If he does not know it, what kind of happiness can there be in the blindness of ignorance? And if he does know it, he can't avoid being afraid of losing that which he knows can be lost. And so a continuous fear prevents him being happy. And if he thinks the possibility of losing it a matter for indifference, then the good whose loss can be borne with such equanimity must be small indeed.

'Furthermore, since you are a man I know to have been fully convinced by innumerable proofs that the human mind cannot die, and since it is clear that happiness which depends on chance comes to an end with the death of the body, it seems beyond doubt that if this happiness dependent on chance can bring pleasure, then the whole human race falls at death into misery. Yet we know that many men have sought the enjoyment of happiness through death and even through suffering and torment. It seems that the happiness which cannot make men unhappy by its cessation, cannot either make them happy by its presence.

'The careful man will wish
To build a lasting home
Unshakeable by winds
That thunder from the East.
He'll shun the open sea
That threatens with its waves,
And choose no mountain peaks
Which all the strength of winds
Buffet and beat from the South;
He'll choose no thirsty sands
That sink and melt away
Beneath the building's weight.
He'll flee the dangerous lot
Of sites that please the eye,
Secure on lowly rock.

Though thunderous winds resound
And churn the seething sea,
Hidden away in peace
And sure of your strong-built walls,
You will lead a life serene
And smile at the raging storm.'

V

'But the applications of reasoning that I have been using on you are beginning to penetrate, and the time has come, I think, for something rather stronger. So then, if the gifts that Fortune offers are not transitory and short-lived, tell me, which is there among them that can ever belong to you or whose worthlessness is not revealed by a moment's thoughtful consideration? What makes riches precious, the fact that they belong to you or some quality of their own? And which is preferable, the gold itself or the power conferred by hoarded wealth? Yet if being miserly always makes men hated, while being generous wins them popularity, it is by spending rather than hoarding that men win the better reputation. Now, if something which is transferred to another cannot remain with its first owner, it is only when money is transferred to others in the exercise of liberality and ceases to be possessed that it becomes valuable. This same money, if it were ever collected together from wherever it is among people into the possession of one man would make all the rest destitute of money. When you speak, your whole voice fills the ears of many hearers to an equal extent, but your riches cannot in the same way be shared equally among many without diminution. When riches are shared among many it is inevitable that they impoverish those from whom they pass. How poor and barren riches really are, then, is clear from the way that it is impossible for many to share them undiminished, or for one man to possess them without reducing all the others to poverty.

'Perhaps your eyes are attracted by the way precious stones

reflect the light. But if there is any special quality in this brilliance, it is in the light of the precious stones, not of men, so that I am astonished that men can admire them. Surely there is nothing devoid of life to give it movement, and devoid of structure, which living rational nature can justifiably consider beautiful? Such things may be works of the Creator and may draw some minimal beauty from their own ornamental nature, but they are of an inferior rank to you as a more excellent creature, and cannot in any way merit your admiration.

'Perhaps, again, you find pleasure in the beauty of the countryside. Creation is indeed very beautiful, and the countryside a beautiful part of creation. In the same way we are sometimes delighted by the appearance of the sea when it's very calm and look up with wonder at the sky, the stars, the moon and the sun. However, not one of these has anything to do with you, and you daren't take credit for the splendour of any of them. The fact that flowers blossom in spring confers no distinction on you, and the swelling fullness of the autumn harvest is no work of yours. You are, in fact, enraptured with empty joys, embracing blessings that are alien to you as if they were your own. I ask you, why? For Fortune can never make yours what Nature has made alien to you. Of course the fruits of the land are appointed as food for living beings; but if you wish only to satisfy your needs – and that is all Nature requires – there is no need to seek an excess from Fortune. Nature is content with few and little: if you try to press superfluous additions upon what is sufficient for Nature, your bounty will become sickening if not harmful.

'Perhaps you think that beauty means being resplendent in clothing of every variety: but if the clothing catches my eye, my admiration will be directed at either the quality of the material or the skill of the tailor. If you take pleasure in having a long line of attendants to wait on you, there are two points to consider: either they are rogues, in which case your household is nothing less than a dangerous burden and a positive threat to its master; or they are honest, and other men's honesty can scarcely be counted among your possessions.

'From all this it is obvious that not one of those things which you count among your blessings is in fact any blessing of yours at all. And if, then, they don't contain a spark of beauty worth seeking, why weep over their loss or rejoice at their preservation? If Nature gives them their beauty, how does it involve you? They would still have been pleasing by themselves, even if separated from your possessions. It isn't because they are part of your wealth that they are precious, but because you thought them precious that you wanted to add them to the sum of your riches.

'What in fact is it that you are looking for in all this outcry against Fortune? To put poverty to flight with plenty? If so, it has turned out the very opposite. The more varied your precious possessions, the more help you need to protect them, and the old saying is proved correct, he who hath much, wants much. And the contrary is true as well, he needs least who measures wealth according to the needs of nature, and not the excesses of ostentation.

'It seems as if you feel a lack of any blessing of your own inside you, which is driving you to seek your blessings in things separate and external. And so when a being endowed with a godlike quality in virtue of his rational nature thinks that his only splendour lies in the possession of inanimate goods, it is the overthrow of the natural order. Other creatures are content with what is their own, but you, whose mind is made in the image of God, seek to adorn your superior nature with inferior objects, oblivious of the great wrong you do your Creator. It was His will that the human race should rule all earthly creatures, but you have degraded yourself to a position beneath the lowest of all. If every good is agreed to be more valuable than whatever it belongs to, then by your own judgement when you account the most worthless of objects as goods[6] of yours, you make yourself lower than those very things, and it is no less than you deserve. Indeed, the condition of human nature is just this; man towers above the rest of creation so long as he recognizes his own nature, and when he forgets it, he sinks lower than the beasts. For other living things to be ignorant of themselves, is natural; but for man it is a defect. What an obvious mistake to make – to think that anything can be enhanced by decoration that does not belong to it. It's impossible. For if there is anything striking in the decoration, that is what is praised, while the veiled and hidden object continues just the same in all its ugliness.

'My contention is that no good thing harms its owner, a thing which you won't gainsay. But wealth very often does harm its owners, for all the most criminal elements of the population who are thereby all the more covetous of other people's property are convinced that they alone are worthy to possess all the gold and precious stones there are. You are shuddering now at the thought of club and knife, but if you had set out on the path of this life with empty pockets, you would whistle your way past any highwayman.[7] How splendid, then, the blessing of mortal riches is! Once won, they never leave you carefree again.

> 'O happy was that long lost age
> Content with nature's faithful fruits
> Which knew not slothful luxury.
> They would not eat before due time
> Their meal of acorns quickly found,
> And did not know the subtlety

6. Boethius uses the Latin word *bonum* with greater freedom than is possible with the corresponding English word 'good'. In translating I have sometimes used the word 'blessing' and sometimes the word 'good'.

7. This is a reminiscence of a famous line of Juvenal (X, 22):

> cantabit vacuus coram latrone viator,

translated by Peter Green (Penguin Classics translation, p. 205): 'The empty-handed traveller whistles his way past any highwayman.'

Of making honey sweeten wine,
Or how the power of Tyrian dyes
Could colour shining flocks[8] of silk.
A grassy couch gave healthy sleep,
A gliding river healthy drink;
The tallest pine-tree gave them shade.
Men did not plunder all the world
And cut a path across the seas
With merchandise for foreign shores.
War horns were silent in those days
And blood unspilt in bitter hate
To horrify the reddening earth.
What reason then for enmity,
To seek the frenzied clash of arms,
When all men saw was gaping wounds
Without return for blood so spilt?
Would that our age could now return
To those pure ways of leading life.
But now the passion to possess
Burns fiercer than Mount Etna's fire.
Alas for the man, whoever he was,
Who first dug heaps of buried gold
And diamonds content to hide,
And gave us perils of such price!'

VI

'I should like to say something about the dignities of high
office and the exercise of power, but I am at a loss because in
your ignorance of the true nature of power and dignities
people like you exalt themselves to high heaven in virtue of
the offices they hold. Now, whenever high office has fallen
into the hands of wicked men, the disaster has been greater
than flood or volcanic eruption. You remember, I am sure,

8. Strictly speaking the word *flocks* (translating Latin *vellera*) is more appropriate to wool than silk; but the Romans were ignorant of the silkworm and
believed that silk was harvested like cotton which was poetically called 'wool
from a tree'. Cf. Virgil, *Georgics*, II, 121.

how (principle of freedom though it had been) your ancestors wanted to abolish the consulship because of the arrogance of the consuls, just as before that the same arrogance had led them to abolish the title of king. If, on the other hand, the very rare case arises when these offices fall to honest men, surely the only aspect of them which finds favour is the honesty of the men who hold the offices. It follows, if this is so, that honour is not accorded to virtue because of the office held, but to the office because of the virtue of the holder.

'However, let us examine this much lauded and much sought after power of yours. You creatures of earth, don't you stop to consider the people over whom you think you exercise authority? You would laugh if you saw a community of mice and one mouse arrogating to himself power and jurisdiction over the others. Again, think of the human body: could you discover anything more feeble than man, when often even a tiny fly can kill him either by its bite or by creeping into some inward part of him? The only way one man can exercise power over another is over his body and what is inferior to it, his possessions. You cannot impose anything on a free mind, and you cannot move from its state of inner tranquillity a mind at peace with itself and firmly founded on reason. The tyrant Nearchus thought he would be able to torture the philosopher Zeno[9] into betraying his fellow conspirators in a plot against his person, but Zeno bit off his tongue and threw it in the face of the enraged tyrant. Nearchus had thought the tortures an occasion for barbarity, but Zeno made them an opportunity for heroism. There is nothing, in fact, which one man can do to another, which he

---

9. Boethius does not give the name of the tyrant or the philosopher: Diogenes Laertius tells the story of Zeno of Elea, who was afterwards pounded to death in a mortar (*Lives of eminent philosophers*, translated by R. D. Hicks, Loeb Classical Library, 1925, IX.5.27. Cf. the reference to the torture of Zeno, p. 39). But he tells a similar story of Anaxarchus of Abdera and the Cypriot tyrant Nicocreon (IX.10.58). According to the scholiast the philosopher concerned was Anaxagoras.

cannot himself suffer at the hands of someone else. We have the story of how the Egyptian king Busiris used to put strangers to death until he himself was killed by a stranger in the person of Hercules.[10] And in the first Punic War your general Regulus put fetters on many a Carthaginian prisoner of war, but not long afterwards was himself holding out his hands to receive a conqueror's chains.[11] Can you, then, consider it power at all, when a man cannot ensure that someone does not inflict on him what he can inflict on others?

'If, furthermore, in these dignities and powers there was some natural and intrinsic good, they would never fall into the hands of evil men, since incompatible things do not usually associate, and nature rejects the combination of opposites. There is no doubt, then, that for the most part it is evil men who hold the offices, and it is therefore clear that these are not intrinsically good, since they admit of being associated with evil men. And the same may be properly concluded in the case of all fortune's gifts, since they fall in greater abundance on all the most wicked people. There is another point to be considered about them. No one doubts that a man in whom he has seen evidence of bravery is brave: a man endowed with speed is manifestly speedy. In the same way music makes a man a musician, medicine makes him a doctor, and rhetoric makes him an orator; for it is the nature of anything to perform the office proper to it. It does not become mixed up in the operations of contrary things and actually repels opposites. But riches are unable to quench insatiable greed; power does not make a man master of himself if he is imprisoned by the indissoluble chains of wicked lusts; and when high office is bestowed on unworthy men, so far from making them worthy, it only betrays them and reveals their unworthiness. The reason for this is that you are accustomed to using

10. The story may be found in Robert Graves's *The Greek Myths* (Penguin Books ed.), 133.k.

11. Cicero, *De Officiis*, III, 99.

the wrong words to refer to things which are by nature otherwise, and are easily proved to be so by their very operation. So neither riches, power nor high office can properly be called by these words. And lastly we may reach the same conclusion about Fortune as a whole. She has nothing worth pursuing, and no trace of intrinsic good; she never associates with good men and does not turn into good men those with whom she does associate.

> 'We know the ruin Nero wrought
> When Rome was fired and great men killed;
> By brother's hand his brother slain,
> He dripped with blood from his mother spilled.
> A practised eye o'er the corpse he rolled
> With never a tear to wet his cheek,
> Cool connoisseur of beauty cold.[12]
> The empire that he held in sway
> From eastern sun's rise then was spread
> To where he sinks at close of day.
> Its northern march where the two Bears stand,
> Its southern bounds where the parched south wind
> Burns and bakes the arid sand.
> Could this high power stretched east and west
> Check Nero's frenzied lunacy?
> Too often Fate, by all abhorred,
> To savage poison adds the sword.'

VII

Then I spoke to her and said that she was well aware of how little I had been governed by worldly ambition. I had sought the means of engaging in politics so that virtue should not grow old unpraised.

'And that,' she replied, 'is the one thing that could entice

12. Boethius refers in this poem to Nero's murder of his stepbrother Britannicus and of his mother Agrippina whose corpse he was reputed to have inspected and praised for its figure. See Tacitus, *The Annals of Imperial Rome*, Penguin Classics ed., pp. 281 and 306–7, and Suetonius, *The Twelve Caesars*, Penguin Classics ed., pp. 226–8.

minds endowed with natural excellence though not yet perfected with the finishing touch of complete virtue – the desire for glory, the thought of being famed for the noblest of services to the state. But consider how thin such fame is and how unimportant. It is well known, and you have seen it demonstrated by astronomers, that beside the extent of the heavens, the circumference of the earth has the size of a point; that is to say, compared with the magnitude of the celestial sphere, it may be thought of as having no extent at all. The surface of the world, then, is small enough, and of it, as you have learnt from the geographer Ptolemy, approximately one quarter is inhabited by living beings known to us. If from this quarter you subtract in your mind all that is covered by sea and marshes and the vast area made desert by lack of moisture, then scarcely the smallest of regions is left for men to live in. This is the tiny point within a point, shut in and hedged about, in which you think of spreading your fame and extending your renown, as if a glory constricted within such tight and narrow confines could have any breadth or splendour. Remember, too, that this same narrow enclosure in which we live is the home of many nations which differ in language, customs and their whole way of life. Because of the difficulty of the journey, the difference of speech and the infrequence of trade, even the renown of great cities does not reach them, let alone the fame of individuals. Cicero mentions somewhere that in his time the fame of Rome had still not penetrated the Caucasus mountains, although the empire was then fully grown and an object of fear to the Parthians and other peoples in the east.[13]

'Surely you see, then, how cramped and confined the fame is which you are toiling to spread and propagate. You cannot

13. Boethius may be thinking of a passage in the *Dream of Scipio* on which this section of the *Consolation* seems to be dependent (*Ciceronis Somnium Scipionis* VI, 13, ed. Meissner – Landgraf, Leipzig 1915, repr. Amsterdam 1964, p. 24; cf. Klingner, op. cit., pp. 9 ff.) or of the *Hortensius* frg. 80/8. For Cicero the Caucasus mountains meant the end of the world.

expect the reputation of one of her citizens to succeed in penetrating regions which the glorious name of Rome cannot reach. And what about the fact that the manners and customs of different peoples are so unalike that different peoples will consider the same thing praiseworthy or punishable? A man may be pleased at the publication of his fame abroad, but among many peoples it may not be to his benefit at all to have his reputation spread. So a man should be content when he is famous throughout his own people, and his bright immortal fame will be confined within the bounds of a single nation.

'Many men have been famous in their time but their memory has perished because there were no historians to write about them. And yet the very histories are of little use when like their authors they become lost in the depths of time which makes all things obscure. When you think of your future fame you think you are creating for yourself a kind of immortality. But if you think of the infinite recesses of eternity you have little cause to take pleasure in any continuation of your name. The span of a single second can be compared with ten thousand years, but minute though it may be, it still has a value in proportion because each is a finite measure of time. But ten thousand years, or any multiple of it however great, cannot be compared with unending eternity. For while finite things can be compared with one another, the finite and the infinite can never be compared. So however protracted the life of your fame, when compared with unending eternity it is shown to be not just little, but nothing at all.

'You, however, don't know how to act uprightly except with an eye to popular favour and empty reputation. You ignore those excellent qualities, a good conscience and virtue, and pursue your reward in the common gossip of people. Listen while I tell you how cleverly someone once ridiculed the shallowness of this kind of conceit. A certain man once made a virulent attack on another man for falsely assuming the title of philosopher more in order to satisfy his overweening pride than to practise virtue, and added that he would accept that the title was justified if the man could suffer attacks upon him with patience and composure. For a time he did assume patience and after accepting the insults asked with a sneer whether the other now agreed that he was a philosopher. "I would," came the reply, "if you had not spoken."[14]

'But it is great men we are considering, men who seek fame for virtue. What do they care about reputation when the body grows lifeless in death which ends all things? If the whole of man dies, body and soul – a belief which our reason forbids us – fame is nothing at all, since the man who is said to have won it doesn't exist. But if the mind stays conscious when it is freed from the earthly prison and seeks out heaven in freedom, surely it will despise every earthly affair. In the experience of heaven it will rejoice in its delivery from earthly things.

> 'Let him whose headstrong thoughts no other end
> Than praise, nor higher purpose contemplate
> Than fame, the width and breadth of heaven regard
> And with the narrow earth their magnitude
> Compare. This narrow circle of the world –
> O shame – his spreading glory cannot fill.
> Why do the proud endeavour to escape
> The destined yoke of man's mortality?
> Fame may diffuse to peoples far remote,
> And as she spreads may loosen tongues of men;
> The house may shine with honours radiant,
> But leveller Death despising glory's pride,
> In scorn of rank abases all alike,
> The mighty to the humble equal made.
> Where now the bones of staunch Fabricius?
> Where lies unbending Cato, Brutus where?
> A little fame lives on inscribed in stone,

14. According to Plutarch (*De vitioso pudore* 532 f in the *Moralia* translated by P. H. de Lacy and B. Einarson, Loeb Classical Library, 1959) Euripides said that the wise man's answer was silence: cf. Proverbs II, 12. 'He who belittles his neighbour lacks sense, but a man of understanding remains silent.'

A line or two of empty reputation:
We know their splendid names but not their selves.
You, too, lie utterly unknown to men,
And no renown can render you well-known:
For if you think that fame can lengthen life
By mortal famousness immortalized,
The day will come that takes your fame as well,
And there a second death for you awaits.'

VIII

'But I don't want you to think I am rigidly opposed to Fortune, for there are times when she stops deceiving and helps man. I mean when she reveals herself, when she throws off her disguise and admits her game. Perhaps you still don't understand what I'm saying. What I want to say is a paradox, and so I am hardly able to put it into words. For bad fortune, I think, is more use to a man than good fortune. Good fortune always seems to bring happiness, but deceives you with her smiles, whereas bad fortune is always truthful because by changing she shows her true fickleness. Good fortune deceives, but bad fortune enlightens. With her display of specious riches good fortune enslaves the minds of those who enjoy her, while bad fortune gives men release through the recognition of how fragile a thing happiness is. And so you can see Fortune in one way capricious, wayward and ever inconstant, and in another way sober, prepared and made wise by the experience of her own adversity. And lastly, by her flattery good fortune lures men away from the path of true good, but adverse fortune frequently draws men back to their true good like a shepherdess with her crook. Do you think it is of small account that this harsh and terrible misfortune has revealed those friends whose hearts are loyal to you? She has shown you the friends whose smiles were true smiles, and those whose smiles were false; in deserting you Fortune has taken her friends with her and left those who are really yours.

Had you remained untouched and, as you thought, blessed by
Fortune, you would have been unable to get such knowledge
at any price. So you are weeping over lost riches when you
have really found the most precious of all riches – friends who
are true friends.

'The world in constant change
Maintains a harmony,
And elements keep peace
Whose nature is to clash.
The sun in car of gold
Draws forth the rosy day,
And evening brings the night
When Luna holds her sway.
The tides in limits fixed
Confine the greedy sea;
No waves shall overflow
The rolling field and lea.
And all this chain of things
In earth and sea and sky
One ruler holds in hand:
If Love relaxed the reins
All things that now keep peace
Would wage continual war
The fabric to destroy
Which unity has formed
With motions beautiful.
Love, too, holds peoples joined
By sacred bond of treaty,
And weaves the holy knot
Of marriage's pure love.
Love promulgates the laws
For friendship's faithful bond.
O happy race of men
If Love who rules the sky
Could rule your hearts as well!'

BOOK III

I

SHE had stopped singing, but the enchantment of her song left me spellbound. I was absorbed and wanted to go on listening. After a moment I spoke to her.

'You are the greatest comfort for exhausted spirits. By the weight of your tenets and the delightfulness of your singing you have so refreshed me that I now think myself capable of facing the blows of Fortune. You were talking of cures that were rather sharp. The thought of them no longer makes me shudder; in fact I'm so eager to hear more, I fervently beg you for them.'

'I knew it,' she replied. 'Once you began to hang on my words in silent attention, I was expecting you to adopt this attitude – or rather, to be more exact, I myself created it in you. The remedies still to come are, in fact, of such a kind that they taste bitter to the tongue, but grow sweet once they are absorbed.

'But you say you are eager to hear more. You would be more than eager if you knew the destination I am trying to bring you to.'

I asked what it was and she told me that it was true happiness.

'Your mind dreams of it,' she said, 'but your sight is clouded by shadows of happiness and cannot see reality.'

I begged her to lead on and show me the nature of true happiness without delay.

'For you,' she said, 'I will do so gladly.

'But first I will try to describe and sketch an idea of the cause of happiness. Then, with a proper vision of that, you will be able to turn your gaze in a different direction and recognize the pattern of true happiness.

'Whoever wants to sow in virgin soil
First frees the fields of undergrowth and bush,
Cuts back thick ferns and brambles with the scythe
And clears the way for crops of swelling wheat.
The tongue that first has tasted bitter food
Finds honey that the bees have won more sweet;
And stars shine out more pleasing to the eye
When from the south the rain winged wind has dropped.
The darkness first the morning star dispels,
Then beauteous day drives in his rosy steeds.
You, too, have seen the face of spurious good
From whose ill yoke you start to raise your neck,
And true good now shall penetrate your mind.'

II

She stood gazing at the ground for a while, as if she had re-
treated into the recesses of thought, and then began to speak
again.

'In all the care with which they toil at countless enterprises,
mortal men travel by different paths, though all are striving to
reach one and the same goal, namely, happiness, which is a
good which once obtained leaves nothing more to be desired.
It is the perfection of all good things and contains in itself all
that is good; and if anything were missing from it, it couldn't
be perfect, because something would remain outside it,
which could still be wished for. It is clear, therefore, that
happiness is a state made perfect by the presence of everything
that is good, a state, which, as we said, all mortal men are
striving to reach though by different paths. For the desire for
true good is planted by nature in the minds of men, only
error leads them astray towards false good.

'Some men believe that perfect good consists in having no
wants, and so they toil in order to end up rolling in wealth.
Some think that the true good is that which is most worthy
of respect, and so struggle for position in order to be held in
respect by their fellow citizens. Some decide that it lies in the

highest power, and either want to be rulers themselves, or try to attach themselves to those in power. Others think that the best thing is fame and busy themselves to make a name in the arts of war or peace. But most people measure the possession of the good by the amount of enjoyment and delight it brings, convinced that being abandoned to pleasure is the highest form of happiness. Others again confuse ends and means with regard to these things, such as people who desire riches for the sake of power and pleasure, or those who want power for the sake of money or fame. So it is in these and other such objectives that the aim of human activity and desire is to be found, in fame and popularity which appear to confer a kind of renown, or in a wife and children which men desire for the sake of the pleasure they give. And as for friendship, the purest kind is counted as a mark not of good fortune, but of moral worth, but all other friendship is cultivated for the sake of power or pleasure.

'Now, it is clear that physical endowments are aspects of higher blessings: for clearly bodily strength and size give a man might; beauty and speed give him renown; and health gives him pleasure. And through all of this it is clear that the only thing men desire is happiness. Each man considers whatever he desires above all else to be the supreme good. We have already defined the supreme good as happiness; so that the state which each man desires above all others is judged by him to be one of happiness. So you have before you the general pattern of human happiness – wealth, position, power, fame, pleasure. Taking only these into consideration, Epicurus with perfect consistency stated that pleasure was the highest good, because all the others bring the mind enjoyment.

'But to return to the pursuits of men. In spite of a clouded memory, the mind seeks its own good, though like a drunkard it cannot find the path home. No one would say that people who strive to have all they want are wrong. In fact there is no other thing which could so successfully create happiness as a condition provided with all that is good, a condition of self-sufficiency and with no wants. No one again would say those people are wrong who think that that which is most worthy of respect and veneration is the best. It is no cheap and contemptible thing the possession of which is the object of the exertions of almost all mankind. Power, too, must be counted among the things that are good. For something which is agreed to be superior to all things can scarcely be considered weak and impotent. And, again, fame can't be considered valueless. It can't be ignored because anything that is of great excellence is also of great renown. It is irrelevant to say that happiness is a state free from anxiety, sadness, and the domination of grief and suffering, when even in small matters, what men look for is something which gives delight by its possession and enjoyment.

'These, then, are the things which people long to obtain. And they want riches, position, estates, glory and pleasures, because it is their conviction that through them they will achieve self-sufficiency, respect, power, celebrity and happiness. This is the good that men are looking for in such a variety of pursuits. And it is not difficult to show the hand of nature in this, since in spite of the variety and difference of their opinions, men are agreed in their choice of the good as their goal.

'My pleasure is to sing with pliant strings
How mighty Nature holds the reins of things,
And how she frames her laws in providence
With which to stabilize the world immense;
How all things singly she doth bind and curb
With such a bond that nothing can disturb.
Although the Punic lion fetters wears
With ornaments, and often lashes bears,
Although he fears the tamer and will take
Such food as outstretched hands an offering make,

If blood should just once touch his bristling jaws,
His latent spirit will return and cause
Him with a roar his old self to recall
And break the chains that from his neck will fall.
First limb from limb the tamer then is torn
Whose new spilt blood augments the rage reborn.
A bird which chattered noisily when free
Into a cage is taken from the tree;
Though cups are set all sweet with honey there
And food in plenty with the sweetest care
Is ministered by men in their delight,
It flutters in the cage and catches sight
Of where the pleasant woodland shade is cast:
The food beneath its feet is scattered fast;
Now for the wood alone she sadly longs,
For the woods alone she sings her whispered songs.
Forced by strong hands the pliant switch obeys,
Its bended head down to the ground it lays;
But when those hands the withy cease to ply,
Its head springs up again to face the sky.
The sun into the western waves descends,
Where underground a hidden way he wends;
Then to his rising in the east he comes:
All things seek the place that best becomes.
Each thing rejoices when this is retrieved:
For nothing keeps the order it received
Except its rising to its fall it bend
And make itself a circle without end.'

III

'You earthly creatures, you also dream of your origin, however faint the vision. You do have some sort of notion, unclear as it is, of the true goal of happiness, and so an instinctive sense of direction actually guides you towards the true good, only various errors lead you astray. Consider, therefore, whether men really can reach their appointed goal by the means with which they think they are going to win happiness. If money or position or the rest do bring some sort of condition which doesn't seem to lack any of the good things, I will join you in admitting that some people do become happy through the possession of them. But if money and the rest can't achieve what they promise and are actually lacking in the greater number of good things, it will be quite obvious that in them men are snatching at a false appearance of happiness.

'So first I will ask you a few questions, since you yourself were a wealthy man not long ago. In the midst of all that great store of wealth, was your mind never troubled by worry arising from a feeling of injury?'

'Yes it was,' I replied; 'in fact I can't remember when my mind was ever free from some sort of worry.'

'And that was either because something was missing which you didn't want to be missing, or because something was present which you would have preferred not to have been present.'

'Yes.'

'You wanted the presence of one thing and the absence of another?'

'Yes.'

'Now a man must be lacking something if he misses it, mustn't he?'

'Yes.'

'And if a man lacks something he is not in every way self-sufficient?'

'No.'

'And so you felt this insufficiency even though you were supplied with wealth?'

'Yes, I did.'

'So that wealth cannot make a man free of want and self-sufficient, though this was the very promise we saw it offering. And this, too, I think, is a point of great importance, namely the fact that money has no inherent property such as to stop it being taken away from those who possess it, against their will.'

I had to agree.

'You can hardly do otherwise,' she continued, 'when it can happen that someone takes it from another against his will because he is stronger. What else are the lawsuits for except to recover moneys that have been stolen by fraud or violence?'

'That is true.'

'So that a man will need outside help to protect his money.'

'Yes.'

'But he won't need it if he doesn't possess any money which may be lost?'

'No.'

'So the situation has been reversed. Wealth which was thought to make a man self-sufficient in fact makes him dependent on outside help. In which case, what is the way in which riches remove want? If you say that rich people do have the means of satisfying hunger and driving away thirst and cold, I will reply that although want can be checked in this way by riches, it can't be entirely removed. Every hungry and clamorous want may be satisfied with the help of riches, but the want which admits of being satisfied necessarily still remains. There is no need for me to mention that nature is satisfied with little, whereas nothing satisfies greed. So that, if so far from being able to remove want, riches create a want of their own, there is no reason for you to believe that they confer self-sufficiency.

> 'Though wanton gold-lust urge the rich man on
> To reap in wealth that cannot sate his greed,
> Though ponderous Persian[1] pearls bow down his head
> And oxen by the score his acres tread,
> Each day he lives with gnawing care he'll ache,
> And dead, his fickle fortunes him forsake.'

1. To the Romans the Persian Gulf and not the Red Sea was known as the *Mare Rubrum*. 'It was commonly believed that in that part of the world the beach was strewn with jewels and pearls cast up by the sea.' (K. F. Smith, *The Elegies of Albus Tibullus*, Darmstadt, 1964, p. 413, note on 2.2., 16.)

IV

'But it is said, when a man comes to high office, that makes him worthy of honour and respect. Surely such offices don't have the power of planting virtue in the minds of those who hold them, do they? Or of removing vices? No: the opposite is true. More often than removing wickedness, high office brings it to light, and this is the reason why we are angry at seeing how often high office has devolved upon the most wicked of men – why Catullus calls Nonius a kind of malignant growth, in spite of the office he held.[2]

'Surely you can see how much disgrace high office heaps upon the evil? If they don't become famous because of appointments to high office, their unworthiness will be less conspicuous. And was it possible that so much danger could lead you, too, at long last to think of taking office along with Decoratus?[3] Surely you could see he had a thoroughly evil mind, the mind of a parasite and informer? We can scarcely consider men worthy of respect on account of the offices they hold, if we judge them unworthy of those offices! But if you saw a man endowed with wisdom, you would hardly think him unworthy of respect or of the wisdom he was endowed with, would you?'

2.   Catullus 52: Quid est, Catulle? quid moraris emori?
                        sella in curuli struma Nonius sedet,
                        per consulatum peierat Vatinius
                        quid est, Catulle? quid moraris emori?
       (Drop dead, Catullus, lie right down where you are and die.
       That blister Nonius occupies a magistrate's chair;
       Vatinius commits perjury – and collects a consulate.
       Drop dead, Catullus, just drop right down and die.
       – Peter Whigham's translation, Penguin Classics ed. p. 111)
   The details of the poem are a little puzzling since the identity of the Nonius in question is unknown and it is uncertain whether the word *struma* (meaning 'a scrofulous tumour') is a pun on Nonius' name or a reference to his illness; to add to the uncertainty, Cicero taunts Vatinius with the same deformity. See C. J. Fordyce, *Catullus, A Commentary*, Oxford, 1961.
   3. Decoratus was quæstor in A.D. 508.

'No.'

'Because virtue has her own individual worth, which she immediately transfers to whoever possesses her. But as public offices cannot do this, it is clear that they have no beauty or worth of their own.

'There is another point we should especially note: if a man is the more worthless the more widely he is despised, then, since high office displays men to the public gaze, but cannot make them worthy of respect, it makes them instead more despised. But not with impunity; for wicked men confer a like return on the offices they hold: they discredit them through contact with themselves.

'But I want you to see how true respect cannot be obtained through the insubstantial honours of high office; take the example of a man who has been consul many times and comes by chance among foreign peoples: would his offices make him respected by them? If it were a natural property of high offices, they would never fail to have this effect anywhere in the world, just as anywhere on earth fire is always hot. But as it is the false opinion of men that connects them with this function and not some inherent property, immediately they reach people who don't consider them honours, they come to nothing.

'This is what happens among foreigners. But do they last for ever in the country of their origin? There was a time when the praetorship was an office of great power, but now it is no more than an empty name and a heavy burden on the pockets of the senatorial class. And once upon a time if a man had charge of the corn supplies, he was considered a great man, but now no office is lower. For as we said just now, if a thing has no beauty of its own, its dignity varies at different times according to the opinion of the people who use it.

'If, therefore, high offices cannot make people worthy of respect and if, furthermore, they become tarnished by contact with evil men; if their splendour can disappear with the change of time and they grow cheap in the estimation of foreign peoples, without asking what beauty they can confer, what beauty worth desiring do they even possess?

> 'Although the proud lord clothed himself
> In purple robes and gem-stones white,
> Yet Nero grew to all men's hate
> A wild and cruel sybarite.
> At times the evil man would give
> To reverend elders office low;
> But who could think those honours good
> Which wretched men on them bestow?'

V

'Can being a king or being the friend of a king give a man power? If the answer is "Yes, because their happiness endures uninterrupted," I shall reply that history, and our own times too, is full of examples of kings who exchanged happiness for ruin. What a splendid thing power is, when we find it insufficient even for its own preservation!

'Now, if kingly power is a source of happiness, any deficiency in it means a diminution of happiness and the introduction of unhappiness, doesn't it? Whatever the size of human empires, it is inevitable that many people are left unruled by any king. And wherever the power that makes men happy comes to an end, lack of power enters and makes them wretched. So that there necessarily exists among kings a larger share of misery. Dionysius the Tyrant of Syracuse knew well enough the dangers of his position, when he illustrated the fears of kingship to Damocles by making a sword dangle over his head by a single hair.

'What is this power, then, which cannot banish the nagging of worry or avoid the pin-prick of fear? Kings would like to live free from worry, but they can't. And then they boast of their power! Do you think of a man as powerful when you see him lacking something which he cannot achieve? A man who goes about with a bodyguard because he is more afraid than the subjects he terrorizes, and whose claim to power depends on the will of those who serve him?

'And what should I say of the friends of kings, when I can show that kingship itself is full of such weakness? They are often brought down while the royal power remains unimpaired, but often too when it collapses. The decision to commit suicide was forced upon Seneca by the very Nero whose friend and mentor he had been. And Papinian who had long been a power in the court was thrown to the soldiers' swords by Caracalla.[4] Each of them was willing to give up his power. Seneca even tried to give his money to Nero and go into retirement. But like men who lose their footing and are pulled down by their own weight, neither was able to achieve what he wanted.

'What sort of power is it, then, that strikes fear into those who possess it, confers no safety on you if you want it, and which cannot be avoided when you want to renounce it? There is no support, either, in friends you acquire because of your good fortune rather than your personal qualities. The friend that success brings you becomes your foe in time of misfortune. And there is no evil more able to do you injury than a friend turned foe.

> 'Whoever wants to wield high power
> Must tame his passions fierce;
> His heart to evil must not cower
> Or bow to lust's fell yoke.

4. Lucius Annaeus Seneca, the Roman philosopher, playwright and *littérateur*, was the boyhood tutor of the emperor Nero, and later on his adviser. He amassed an immense fortune which he offered to the emperor when he asked to be allowed to retire, but Nero refused and later ordered him to commit suicide. He died in A.D. 65. See Tacitus, *Annals*, XIV, 54, Penguin Classics edition (*Annals of Imperial Rome*) pp. 327 ff. Aemilius Papinianus, one of the greatest of the Roman jurists, was executed by the emperor Caracalla in A.D. 212. *Vita Caracallae* 8, 1 ff. in *Scriptores Historiae Augustae* II translated by David Magie, Loeb Classical Library, 1924.

For distant India tremble may
　　Beneath your mighty rule,
And Thulé[5] bow beneath your sway
　　Far in the Northern sea,
But if to care and want you're prey,
　　No king are you, but slave.'

VI

'Fame, in fact, is a shameful thing, and so often deceptive.
Euripides was right to make Andromache cry out

O Fame, o Fame! – many a man ere this
Of no account hast thou set up on high.[6]

Many, indeed, are the men who have wrongly acquired fame
through the false opinions of the people. There is nothing
more conceivably shameful than that. Men who are un-
justifiably commended cannot but blush at the praise they
receive. And even if the praise is deserved, it cannot add
anything to the philosopher's feelings: he measures happiness
not by popularity, but by the true voice of his own conscience.

'If it is thought a fine achievement to have spread this fame
far and wide, it follows that it must be judged shameful not
to have spread one's fame. But, as I said just now, there must
of necessity be many peoples to whom the reputation of one
single man can never extend, so that you may consider a man
famous, whom the next quarter of the globe will never even
have heard of. This is why I don't consider popularity worth
mentioning in this list; its acquisition is fortuitous and its
retention continuously uncertain.

'As for the claim to nobility, no one is blind to the vanity
and worthlessness of that. If it derives from fame, it is

---

5. To the Romans Thulé, variously identified as Iceland or Mainland in the
Shetland Isles, marked the extreme northern limit of the known world, just
as India here stands for the farthest east.

6. *Andromache*, 319.

borrowed nobility, for it is clearly a kind of praise derived from the deeds of one's parents. Fame is the product of praise, and it is logical that it is those who are praised that become famous. Therefore the praise of someone else cannot ennoble you unless you are famous in your own right. If there is anything good in nobility, I think it is only this: that there is a necessary condition imposed upon the noble not to fall short of the virtue of their ancestors.

> 'From one beginning rises all mankind;
> For one Lord rules and fathers all things born.
> He gave the sun his light, the moon her horns,
> And men to earth and stars to grace the sky;
> He closed in bodies minds brought down from high,
> A noble origin for mortal men.
> Why then proclaim your kin and ancestry?
> Look whence you came and see who made you, God.
> No man degenerate is unless through sin
> He leaves his proper source for meaner things.'

VII

'Of bodily pleasure I can think of little to say. Its pursuit is full of anxiety and its fulfilment full of remorse. Frequently, like a kind of reward for wickedness, it causes great illness and unbearable pain for those who make it their source of enjoyment. I do not know what happiness lies in its passions, but that the end of pleasure is sorrow is known to everyone who cares to recall his own excesses. But if bodily pleasure can produce happiness, there is no need to deny that animals are happy, since their whole aim in life is directed towards the fulfilment of bodily needs. The pleasures derived from a wife and children are indeed most honest; but there is a story all too natural that a certain man found his children tormentors. How painful the condition of every such man is, there is no need to remind you, since you have experienced such conditions yourself, and are still not free from anxiety. So I agree with my Euripides when he said that the childless man was fortunate in his misfortune.[7]

> 'One quality alike all pleasures have:
>   They drive their devotees with goads.
> And like a swarm of bees upon the wing,
>   They first pour out their honey loads,
> Then turn and strike their victim's heart
>   And leave behind their deep set sting.'

VIII

'There is no doubt, then, that these roads to happiness are side-tracks and cannot bring us to the destination they promise. The evils with which they are beset are great, as I will briefly show you. If you try to hoard money, you will have to take it by force. If you want to be resplendent in the dignities of high office, you will have to grovel before the man who bestows it: in your desire to outdo others in high honour you will have to cheapen and humiliate yourself by begging. If you want power, you will have to expose yourself to the plots of your subjects and run dangerous risks. If fame is what you seek, you will find yourself on a hard road, drawn this way and that until you are worn with care. Decide to lead a life of pleasure, and there will be no one who will not reject you with scorn as the slave of that most worthless and brittle master, the human body.

'For think how puny and fragile a thing men strive to possess when they set the good of the body before them as their aim. As if you could surpass the elephant in size, the bull in strength, or the tiger in speed! Look up at the vault of heaven: see the strength of its foundation and the speed of its movement, and stop admiring things that are worthless. Yet

7. The source of the quotation is Euripides' *Andromache* (the play already quoted from by Boethius in ch. VI), line 420.

the heavens are less wonderful for their foundation and speed than for the order that rules them.[8]

'The sleek looks of beauty are fleeting and transitory, more ephemeral than the blossom in spring. If, as Aristotle said, we had the piercing eyesight of the mythical Lynceus[9] and could see right through things, even the body of an Alcibiades,[10] so fair on the surface, would look thoroughly ugly once we had seen the bowels inside. Your own nature doesn't make you look beautiful. It is due to the weak eyesight of the people who see you. Think how excessive this desire for the good of the body is, when, as you know, all that you admire can be reduced to nothing by three days of burning fever.

8. This passage must be understood in terms of the Ptolemaic explanation of the universe which was generally accepted from the second century A.D. until the time of Copernicus. According to this theory the universe was geocentric. The earth was surrounded by a series of concentric transparent spheres in each of which was fixed one of the 'seven planets', viz. the Moon, Mercury, Venus, the Sun, Mars, Jupiter and Saturn. (Uranus, Neptune and Pluto were not discovered until the eighteenth century and later.) Beyond the sphere of Saturn lay the sphere of the fixed stars, and beyond that the *Primum Mobile*, which is caused by God to rotate on its own axis once in every twenty-four hours, the speed of the rotation being very high on account of the vast size of the sphere. As it rotates the *Primum Mobile* communicates its motion to the sphere lying contiguous to it, which is thus moved in the same direction, but at a slower speed; the motion of the sphere of the fixed stars is communicated in turn to the sphere of Saturn, and so it progresses through the other six spheres. In this way the observable motions of the heavenly bodies were accounted for, though the Aristotelian account, with which Boethius was acquainted, and the full details of the Ptolemaic account are much more complex, than this brief outline. (See for the Ptolemaic system A. C. Crombie, *Augustine to Galileo*, Mercury Books no. 3, pp. 82 ff. and for Aristotle, W. D. Ross, *Aristotle*, London, 1923 etc., pp. 96–7.) It is the abstract mathematical complexity of the system which regulates the movements of the planets which Boethius finds really wonderful, not just the physical construction of the universe or the immense speed of its rotation.

9. Lynceus was one of the Argonauts, who was supposed to have such sharp eyes that he could see in the dark and discover the whereabouts of hidden treasure. See Robert Graves, *The Greek Myths*, ii, p. 246.

10. Alcibiades, an Athenian military leader of the late fifth century B.C. was famous for his wealth and beauty and notorious for the use he made of them. A good picture of this brilliant but dissolute man is given in Plato's *Symposium* (translated by W. Hamilton in the Penguin Classics).

'The sum of all this is that because they can neither produce the good they promise nor come to perfection by the combination of all good, these things are not the way to happiness and cannot by themselves make people happy.

'Alas, how men by blindness led
  Go from the path astray.
Who looks on spreading boughs for gold,
  On vines for jewels gay?
Who hides his nets on mountain tops
  For a board with fish high piled?
Who sails his boat upon the sea
  To hunt the she-goat wild?
The very ocean's depths men know
  Beneath the waves on high;
They know which strand is rich with pearls,
  Which shores with purple dye;
They know the bays for tender fish,
  For shellfish where to try.
But in their blindness men know not
  Where lies the good they seek:
That which is higher than the sky
  On earth below they seek.
What can I wish you foolish men?
  Wealth and fame pursue,
And when your toil false good has won,
  Then may you see the true!'

IX

'I have said enough to give a picture of false happiness, and if you can see that clearly, the next thing is to show what true happiness is like.'

'I do indeed see that sufficiency has nothing to do with riches, or power with kingship, respect with honours, glory with fame, or happiness with pleasures.'

'But have you grasped the reasons for this?'

'I think I can see a glimmer of them, but I would like to learn of them more clearly from you.'

'The reason is very clear. That which is one and undivided is mistakenly subdivided and removed by men from the state of truth and perfection to a state of falseness and imperfection. Do you consider self-sufficiency as a state deficient in power?'

'Not at all.'

'Of course not; for if a being had some weakness in some respect, it would necessarily need the help of something else.'

I agreed.

'So that self-sufficiency and power are of one and the same nature.'

'So it seems.'

'Would you then consider a being of this kind beneath contempt, or on the contrary supremely worthy of veneration?'

'The latter, there is no doubt about it.'

'Then let us add the state of being revered to sufficiency and power, that we may judge all three to be one.'

'We must, if we care to admit the truth.'

'What do you think, then, would such a combination be unrecognized and unknown, or famous and renowned? Granted that it lacks nothing, possesses all power, and is supremely worthy of honour, ask yourself whether it would lack a glory which it cannot provide for itself and therefore whether it seems of qualified merit.'

'I can only say that in view of its nature it would be unsurpassed in glory.'

'And consequently we may say that glory is no different from the three we already have.'

'Yes.'

'If there were, then, a being self-sufficient, able to accomplish everything from its own resources, glorious and worthy of reverence, surely it would also be supremely happy?'

'How any sorrow could approach such a being is inconceivable: it must be admitted that provided the other qualities are permanent, it will be full of happiness.'

'And for the same reason this conclusion, too, is inescapable; sufficiency, power, glory, reverence and happiness differ in name but not in substance.'

'Yes.'

'Human perversity, then, makes divisions of that which by nature is one and simple, and in attempting to obtain part of something which has no parts, succeeds in getting neither the part – which is nothing – nor the whole, which they are not interested in.'

'How does that happen?'

'If a man pursues wealth by trying to avoid poverty, he is not working to get power; he prefers being unknown and unrecognized, and even denies himself many natural pleasures to avoid losing the money he has got. But certainly no sufficiency is achieved this way, since he is lacking in power and vexed by trouble; he is of no account because of his low esteem, and is buried in obscurity. And if a man pursues only power, he expends wealth, despises pleasures and honour without power, and holds glory of no account. But you can see how much this man also lacks; at any one time he lacks the necessaries of life and is consumed by worry, from which he cannot free himself, so he ceases to be what he most of all wants to be, that is, powerful. A similar argument can be applied to honour, glory, and pleasures, for, since any one of them is the same as the others, a man who pursues one of them to the exclusion of the others, cannot even acquire the one he wants.'

'But suppose someone should want to obtain them all at one and the same time.'

'Then he would be seeking the sum of happiness. But do you think he would find it among these things which we have shown to be unable to confer what they promise?'

'No, I don't.'

'So that it is impossible to find happiness among these things which are thought to confer each of the desired states individually?'

'I agree, and no truer word could be spoken.'

'Then there you have both the nature and the cause of false happiness. Now turn your mind's eye in the opposite direction and you will immediately see the true happiness that I promised.'

'Even a blind man could see it,' I said, 'and you revealed it just now when you were trying to show the causes of false happiness. For unless I'm mistaken, true and perfect happiness is that which makes a man self-sufficient, strong, worthy of respect, glorious and joyful. And to show you that I have more than a superficial understanding, without a shadow of doubt I can see that happiness to be true happiness which, since they are all the same thing, can truly bestow any one of them.'

'You are blessed in this belief, my child, provided you add one thing.'

'What is that?'

'Do you think there is anything among these mortal and degenerate things which could confer such a state?'

'No, I don't, and you have proved it as well as anyone could wish.'

'Clearly, therefore, these things offer man only shadows of the true good, or imperfect blessings, and cannot confer true and perfect good.'

'Yes.'

'Since then you have realized the nature of true happiness and seen its false imitations, what remains now is that you should see where to find this true happiness.'

'Which is the very thing I have long and eagerly been waiting for.'

'But since in the *Timaeus* my servant Plato was pleased to

ask for divine help even over small matters,[11] what do you think we ought to do now in order to be worthy of discovering the source of that supreme good?'

'We ought to pray to the Father of all things. To omit to do so would not be laying a proper foundation.'

'Right,' she said, and immediately began the following hymn.

> 'O Thou who dost by everlasting reason rule,
> Creator of the planets and the sky, who time
> From timelessness didst bring, unchanging Mover,
> No cause drove Thee to mould unstable matter, but
> 5 The form benign of highest good within Thee set.
> All things Thou bringest forth from Thy high archetype:
> Thou, height of beauty, in Thy mind the beauteous world
> Dost bear, and in that ideal likeness shaping it,
> Dost order perfect parts a perfect whole to frame.
> 10 The elements by harmony Thou dost constrain,
> That hot to cold and wet to dry are equal made,
> That fire grow not too light, or earth too fraught with weight.
> The bridge of threefold nature madest Thou soul, which spreads
> Through nature's limbs harmonious and all things moves.
> 15 The soul once cut, in circles two its motion joins,
> Goes round and to itself returns encircling mind,
> And turns in pattern similar the firmament.
> From causes like Thou bringst forth souls and lesser lives,
> Which from above in chariots swift Thou dost disperse
> 20 Through sky and earth, and by Thy law benign they turn
> And back to Thee they come through fire that brings them home.
> Grant, Father, that our minds Thy august seat may scan,
> Grant us the sight of true good's source, and grant us light
> That we may fix on Thee our mind's unblinded eye.
> 25 Disperse the clouds of earthly matter's cloying weight;
> Shine out in all Thy glory; for Thou art rest and peace

11. Before embarking on his account of how the universe began Timaeus says they must pray to all the gods and goddesses, for 'everyone with the least sense always calls on god at the beginning of any undertaking, small or great'. (Plato, *Timaeus* 27C, tr. H. D. P. Lee, Penguin Classics, p. 40.)

To those who worship Thee; to see Thee is our end,
Who art our source and maker, lord and path and goal.'[12]

12. This poem, remarkable for the masterly succinctness of its majestic poetry, has long been regarded as a kind of epitome of the first part of Plato's *Timaeus*, and was especially dear to commentators of the early Middle Ages whose direct knowledge of Plato was otherwise confined to a translation of the *Timaeus* by Chalcidius. There are a number of points, however, in which the Boethian version differs from the *Timaeus* which cannot, therefore, be regarded as its only source. The epitome begins at line 4, and the following parallels with H. D. P. Lee's translation of the *Timaeus* are noteworthy: line 6, Lee, p. 42; 9, Lee, p. 44; 10–12, Lee, pp. 43–4; 13–14, Lee, pp. 49 and 46; 15–16, Lee, pp. 48, 45 and 49; 18, Lee, p. 57; 19, Lee, ibid; 20 and 21, Lee, pp. 57–8. For most of the passages for which there is no parallel in the *Timaeus* sources can be found in the writings of the Neoplatonists and especially Proclus' commentary on the *Timaeus*. The poem, in fact, is composed in the form of a Platonic hymn to God, and is full of phrases which echo the vocabulary of the Platonic hymns. There is also some influence from the Judaeo-Christian tradition, particularly in the movement of the final lines of the poem: the introduction of the particle *for* in line 26 parallels the construction of the *Gloria* in the liturgy of the Western church and the Lord's Prayer rather than the Platonic hymns. And no one can be deaf to the echo in the final line of St John's gospel.

The following phrases need a word of comment:

ll. 7–8. Nowhere does Plato say that God carries the model of the universe in his mind; this is part of the teaching of Neo-platonism.

l. 16. 'encircling mind'. Plato does not say that the soul encircles mind. Plotinus, however, uses the figure of the dance of the imperfect around the perfect, i.e. of created soul around the uncreated mind of God.

l. 17. 'in pattern similar'. Proclus speaks of Soul as set between Mind and Body; soul is moved by Mind, i.e. God, which in a similar way itself moves Body, i.e. corporeal and concrete nature – here the firmament.

l. 18. 'lesser lives'. Proclus commenting on *Timaeus* 41d holds that there are three different kinds of souls; the 'lesser lives' of this passage are either souls enclosed in earthly bodies, or, lesser souls compared with the world soul described in lines 15–17.

ll. 19–21 contain a summary of Neo-platonic religion, the descent of the souls (figuratively spoken of as fixed in chariots in a formula taken over by the Neo-Platonists from Plato himself) from God and their ultimate ascent and return through the purifying action of fire which returns them to God.

Even, therefore, in the part of Boethius' hymn which has been seen as an epitome of the *Timaeus*, Boethius is heavily influenced by the doctrine and sacred hymns of Neo-platonism. For details see Friedrich Klingner, *De Boethii Consolatione Philosophiae*, 2te Unveranderte Auflage, Weidmann, Zurich/Dublin, 1966, pp. 38–67. And for Boethius' use of Proclus' commentary on the *Timaeus*, H. R. Patch in *Speculum* VIII, 1933, pp. 41–51.

X

'Since, then, you have seen the form both of imperfect and of perfect good, I think we now have to show where this perfect happiness is to be found.

'The first question to ask is, I think, whether any good of the kind I defined a moment ago can exist in the natural world. This will prevent our being led astray from the truth of the matter before us by false and ill-founded reasoning. But the existence of this good and its function as a kind of fountain-head of all good things cannot be denied; for everything that is said to be imperfect is held to be so by the absence of perfection. So that if a certain imperfection is visible in any class of things, it follows that there is also a proportion of perfection in it. For if you do away with perfection, it is impossible to imagine how that which is held to be imperfect could exist. The natural world did not take its origin from that which was impaired and incomplete, but issues from that which is unimpaired and perfect and then degenerates into this fallen and worn out condition. But we showed just now that there is a certain imperfect happiness in perishable good, so that there can be no doubt that a true and perfect happiness exists.'

'Which is a very sound and true conclusion,' I said.

'As to where it is to be found, then, you should think as follows. It is the universal understanding of the human mind that God, the author of all things, is good. Since nothing can be conceived better than God, everyone agrees that that which has no superior is good. Reason shows that God is so good that we are convinced that His goodness is perfect. Otherwise He couldn't be the author of creation. There would have to be something else possessing perfect goodness over and above God, which would seem to be superior to Him and of greater antiquity. For all perfect things are obviously superior to those that are imperfect. Therefore, to avoid an unending argument, it must be admitted that the supreme God is to the highest degree filled with supreme and perfect goodness. But we have agreed that perfect good is true happiness; so that it follows that true happiness is to be found in the supreme God.'

'I accept that. There is nothing in any way open to contradiction.'

'But,' she said, 'I must ask you to make sure that your approval of our statement that the supreme God is to the highest degree filled with supreme good is unqualified and final.'

'How do you mean?' I asked.

'By avoiding the assumption that this Father of creation has received this supreme good with which He is said to be filled from outside Himself, or that He possesses it by nature but in such a way as would lead you to suppose that the substance[13] of God the possessor was a separate thing from the

---

13. The application of the word 'substance' in this passage may seem strange. It is, in fact, a technical term of Aristotelian metaphysics, denoting the individual thing about which assertions can be made. For Aristotle, a substance is simply a real thing which actually exists, but since in his view matter is something negative without proper characteristics of its own, that which makes things definite and distinguishable is their form. 'The sensible individuals cannot be defined owing to the material element in them, which renders them perishable and makes them obscure to our knowledge. On the other hand, substance is primarily the definable essence or form of a thing, the principle in virtue of which the material element is some definite concrete object. It follows from this that substance is primarily form which is, in itself, immaterial, so that if Aristotle begins by asserting that individual sensible objects are substances, the course of his thought carries him on towards the view that pure form alone is truly and primarily substance. But the only forms that are really independent of matter are God, the Intelligences of the spheres and the active intellect in man, so that it is these forms which are primarily substance.' (Copleston, op. cit., I, ii, p. 48.) This teaching is alluded to by Boethius in his tractate On the Trinity, where he adds, 'When we say God, we seem to denote a substance; but it is a substance that is supersubstantial.' (Loeb Classical Library ed., p. 17.) The same sort of language is, of course, met with in the Nicene Creed where the Son is said to be of one substance with the Father.

substance of the happiness He possesses. If you thought that He received it from outside Himself, you would be able to count the giver superior to the receiver. But we are in agreement that it is right to consider God the most excellent of things.

'On the other hand, if goodness is a natural property of God, but something logically distinct from Him, whenever we speak of God as the author of creation, an able mind might be able to imagine the existence of a power responsible for bringing together the two that were separate.

'Finally, if one thing is distinct from another, it cannot be the thing from which it is perceived to be distinct. So that which by its own nature is something distinct from supreme good, cannot be supreme good; but this is something we may not hold about Him to whom we agree there is nothing superior. It is impossible for anything to be by nature better than that from which it is derived. I would therefore conclude with perfect logic that that which is the origin of all things is in its own substance supreme good.'

'Perfectly right.'

'But we have agreed that supreme good is the same as happiness.'

'Yes.'

'So that we have to agree that God is the essence of happiness.'

'Your premises are incontestable and I see that this inference follows upon them.'

'Then consider whether this, too, can be firmly accepted: that it is impossible for two supreme goods to exist separate from one another. For it is clear that if the two goods are separate, the one cannot be the other, so that neither could be perfect when each is lacking to the other. But that which is not perfect is obviously not supreme. It is therefore impossible for there to be two separate supreme goods. However, we deduced that both happiness and God are supreme goodness, so that it follows that supreme happiness is identical with supreme divinity.'

'There could scarcely be a conclusion more true to reality, or more sure in its reasoning, or more worthy of God.'

'I will add something to it. Just as in geometry some additional inference may be drawn from a theorem that has been proved, called in technical language, in Greek a *porisma* and in Latin a corollary, I too will give you a kind of corollary. Since it is through the possession of happiness that people become happy, and since happiness is in fact divinity, it is clear that it is through the possession of divinity that they become happy. But by the same logic as men become just through the possession of justice, or wise through the possession of wisdom, so those who possess divinity necessarily become divine. Each happy individual is therefore divine. While only God is so by nature, as many as you like may become so by participation.'

'What you say is beautiful and valuable, whether you give it the Greek or the Latin name.'

'But the most beautiful thing is what logic leads us to add to all this.'

'What is that?'

'Are all the many things we see included under the word happiness like parts combining to form a single body, yet separate in their variety, or is there any one of them which can fully supply the essence of happiness and under which the others may be classed?'

'Could you clarify the question by being more specific?'

'Well, we consider happiness something good, don't we?'

'Yes, the supreme good.'

'You could say the same of all of them. Absolute sufficiency is judged to be the same as happiness, and so too are power, reverence, glory and pleasure. Well, the question is this, all these things – sufficiency, power and the others – are they good as if happiness were a body of which they were members, or is goodness a kind of heading to which they belong?'

'I understand the question which you are proposing we should ask, but I should like to hear what your answer would be.'

'This is how I would resolve it. If all these were related to happiness like limbs to a body, they would differ from one another, because it is the nature of parts that the body is one, but the parts that make it up are diverse. But all these things have been proved to be identical. So that they are not like limbs. Moreover it would appear that happiness was a body made up of a single limb, which is impossible.'

'There is no doubt of that; but I am eager for what is to come.'

'It is clear that the other properties are classed under good. It is just because sufficiency is judged a good that people want it, and it is just because it too is believed to be a good that power is sought after. And exactly the same conclusion may be reached about reverence, glory and pleasure.

'The chief point and reason, therefore, for seeking all things is goodness. For it is quite impossible for that which contains no good in itself whether real or apparent, to be an object of desire. On the other hand, things which are not good by nature are sought after if they nevertheless seem as if they were truly good.

'The result is, therefore, that there is justice in the belief that goodness is the chief point upon which the pursuit of everything hinges and by which it is motivated. What seems most to be desired is the thing that motivates the pursuit of something, as, for example, if a man wants to go riding for the sake of health; it is not so much the motion of horse-riding he desires as the resultant good health. Since, therefore, all things are desired for the sake of the good in them, no one desires them as much as the good itself. But we are agreed that the reason for desiring things is happiness. So that it is patently obvious that the good itself and happiness are identical.'

'I can see no reason for anyone to disagree.'

'But we have shown that God and happiness are one and the same thing.'

'Yes.'

'We may safely conclude, then, that God is to be found in goodness itself and nowhere else.

> 'Come hither now all you who captive are,
> Whom false desire enchains in wicked bonds,
> Desire that makes her home in earthly minds;
> Here will you find release from grievous toil,
> Here find a haven blessed with peaceful calm,
> An ever open refuge from distress.
> Not all the gold that Tagus' sands bestow,
> That Hermus from his glittering banks casts up,
> Or Indus, on whose torrid shores are strewn
> Green emeralds intermixed with dazzling pearls,
> May sharpen and make bright the intellect,
> But wealth in its own darkness clouds the thoughts.
> For all that thus excites and charms the mind
> Dim earth has fostered in her caverns deep;
> While that bright light which rules and animates
> The sky, will shun such dark and ruined souls:
> Whoever once shall see this shining light
> Will say the sun's own rays are not so bright.'

XI

'I agree, for all that you have said is established and connected by the soundest of reasoning.'

Then she asked, 'How valuable would you think it if you could come to know the good itself?'

'Infinitely valuable,' I said, 'if I should also be able to see God, who is the good.'

'I will make it clear with unimpeachable reasoning,' she said, 'provided our recent conclusions may stand.'

'They may,' I said.

'We have proved, then, haven't we, that the various things that the majority of men pursue are not perfect and good, for the reason that they differ from one another, and because they are lacking to one another and cannot confer full and perfect good. On the other hand, true good does come about when they are brought together into one form and efficient power, as it were, so that sufficiency becomes identical with power, reverence, glory and pleasure; unless all are one and the same thing they have no claim to be included among worthwhile objects of pursuit.'

'You have proved it and there is no room at all for doubt.'

'When these objects differ, they're not good, but when they begin to be one they become good; so it comes about that it is through the acquisition of unity that these things are good, doesn't it?'

'It seems so.'

'But do you or do you not agree that everything that is good is so through participation in goodness?'

'I do agree.'

'Then you are obliged to agree by the same argument that unity and goodness are identical. For things whose natural effect is identical must have the same substance in common.'

'I cannot gainsay it.'

'You know, then, that everything that is remains and subsists just so long as it is one, but perishes and dissolves immediately it ceases to be one?'

'How is that?'

'It is just as with living creatures: when soul and body come together and remain united, we speak of a living being, but when this unity breaks up through the separation of either component, it is clear that the living being perishes and no longer exists. The very body, too, so long as it remains in one form through the combination of its members, you see a human figure; but if the parts are divided up and separated and the body's unity destroyed, it ceases to be what it was. You may run through every other thing and it will be clear beyond a shadow of doubt that everything subsists as long as it is one, but perishes when its unity ceases.'

'Yes, I can think of many things of which this is true.'

'Now is there anything which in the course of its natural activity loses the will to exist and desires to obtain death and corruption?'

'If I confine my thoughts to living creatures endowed by nature with freedom of choice, I can find nothing which in the absence of external compulsion would give up the intention to live and willingly hasten towards death. For every kind of animal is at pains to guard its own safety, and shuns death and destruction. But in the case of plants and trees, I am in some doubt as to what I would agree with.'

'And yet there is no room for indecision here either, because you can see how in the first place plants and trees grow up in places suitable to them and where it would be unnatural for them quickly to wither and die. Some grow in fields, some on hills, some in marshes; some cling to rocky ground and the barren desert abounds with others. And if you tried to transplant them into other habitats, they would wither away. Nature gives each one whatever suits it, and as long as life is possible toils to prevent them dying. Just think how they all draw nourishment through their roots, as if they were burying their mouths in the earth, and how strength spreads through their pith and bark. And how the softest part like the pith is always buried inside, while the covering of bark with the strength of the wood is set on the outside to withstand the inclemency of the weather, like a protector capable of enduring such malice. And how painstaking Nature is to ensure that all things are propagated by the multiplication of their seed. Everyone knows that they are like a kind of machine not only for the duration of their own lifetime, but for the almost everlasting propagation of their species.

'Even things which are believed to be inanimate also desire in a similar way that which is their own, don't they? Otherwise why is flame carried upwards by its lightness and solid things carried down by their weight, except because these positions and motions suit the individual things? Furthermore, that which is suitable to each thing, they preserve, just as they destroy what is harmful. Things that are hard, like stone, cohere with great tenacity throughout their parts and resist being easily broken up. But fluids, like air and water, easily give way before a dividing force, and easily reunite again with the parts that have been cut off; and fire doesn't admit of being cut at all.

'We are not dealing with willed motions of the conscious mind, but with instinctive motions, like the way we digest the food we have taken without thinking about it, and the way we breathe in our sleep without being conscious of it. Not even in living things is the love of self-preservation due to the wishes of their mind, but to the principles of their nature. For often when there are reasons which force death upon a creature, Nature turns away in horror, but the will accepts it. And on the other hand, the work of procreation which alone gives mortal creatures their continuity and which Nature always desires, is sometimes curbed by the will. To such an extent does this love of self-preservation stem not from conscious desire, but from natural instinct. Providence has given its creatures one great reason to go on living, namely the instinctive desire for the greatest possible self-preservation. There is no reason, therefore, for you to have any doubt that all things have an instinctive desire to preserve their life and avoid destruction.'

'I admit that what just now seemed uncertain to me I can now see without any doubt.'

'Now, whatever seeks to subsist and remain alive desires to be one; take unity away from a thing and existence too ceases.'

'That is true.'

'So that all things desire unity.'

'Yes.'

'But we proved that unity is identical with goodness.'

'Yes.'

'So that all things seek the good, which you could describe by saying that it is goodness itself which all things desire.'

'No truer conclusion could be discovered. For either all things are inclined to no one thing and will wander about aimlessly as though destitute of any head or helmsman to guide them, or if there is something to which all things are inclined, it will be the sum of all good.'

'I am very happy, my son, for you have fixed in your mind the very mark of the central truth. And in this you have revealed the very thing you were just now saying you did not know.'

'What was that?'

'What the end of all things was. For certainly it is the same as that which all things desire; we have deduced that that is goodness, and so we must agree that the end of all things is the good.

'Whoever deeply searches out the truth
And will not be deceived by paths untrue,
Shall turn unto himself his inward gaze,
Shall bring his wandering thoughts in circle home
5 And teach his heart that what it seeks abroad
It holds in its own treasure chests within.
What error's gloomy clouds have veiled before
Will then shine clearer than the sun himself.
Not all its light is banished from the mind
10 By body's matter which makes men forget.

The seed of truth lies hidden deep within,
And teaching fans the spark to take new life;
Why else unaided can man answer true,
Unless deep in the heart the touchwood burns?
15 And if the muse of Plato speaks the truth,
Man but recalls what once he knew and lost.'[14]

XII

Then I said, 'I agree very strongly with Plato. This is the second time you have reminded me of these matters. The first time was because I had lost the memory through the influence of the body, and this second time because I lost it when I became overwhelmed by the weight of my grief.'

'If you look at what we have already agreed, you won't be far from remembering what you said you did not know just now.'

'What was that?'

'The manner in which the world is governed.'

14. In two dialogues Plato shows that learning is not just the simple process of being instructed by a teacher, but of being helped to 'bring up from within' knowledge which the soul has learned before birth and has then forgotten. In the *Meno* 82B ff. it is demonstrated by the famous experiment with the slave-boy who is helped to solve geometrical problems by himself without being instructed. His soul must have learned geometry (and everything else) before he was born into this life, and in solving the geometrical problems he is simply recalling that knowledge which he had forgotten. (See Plato, *Protagoras and Meno*, Penguin Classics, pp. 129 ff.)

Lines 13-14 of this metre echo a passage in the other dialogue, the *Phaedo* 73A (Plato, *The Last Days of Socrates*, Penguin Classics, p. 121):

'One very good argument,' said Cebes [sc. that what we call learning is just the recollection of knowledge acquired before birth and then forgotten] 'is that when people are asked questions, if the question is put in the right way, they can give a perfectly correct answer, which they could not possibly do unless they had some knowledge and a proper grasp of the subject [sc. acquired before birth].'

Book V poem 3 refers again to the theory that learning is only anamnesis or the reawakening of memory.

'I remember admitting my ignorance, but even though I have some inkling of them I should like to hear more plainly what arguments you would adduce.'

'Just now you thought it was beyond doubt that this world was ruled by God.'

'I still do think it is beyond doubt, and will always think so. I will briefly explain the arguments which convince me in this matter.

'This world would never have coalesced into one form out of such diverse and antagonistic parts had there not been one who could unify such diversity. Their very diversity in turn would make them break out into dissension and tear apart and destroy the unity of the world unless there were a power capable of holding together what he had once woven. Nature's fixed order could not proceed on its path and the various kinds of change could not exhibit motions so orderly in place, time, effect, distance from one another, and nature, unless there was one unmoving and stable power to regulate them. For this power, whatever it is, through which creation remains in existence and in motion, I use the word which all people use, namely God.'

Then she said, 'Since this is your opinion, I think little remains for me to do before you acquire happiness and return safe and sound to your true homeland.

'But let us look at the arguments we have set forth. Under happiness we have included sufficiency, haven't we, and we have agreed that God is happiness itself?'

'Yes.'

'So that in regulating the universe He will need no external assistance – otherwise, if He needs anything, He won't have complete sufficiency.'

'The inference is inescapable.'

'So that He regulates all things by Himself?'

'It cannot be denied.'

'Now, we have proved that God is the good itself.'

'Yes, I remember.'

'So that it is by goodness that He rules all things, since He rules them by Himself and we have agreed that He is the good. It is this which is the helm and rudder, so to speak, by which the fabric of the universe is kept constant and unimpaired.'

'I strongly agree; and this is exactly what I thought you were going to say, although I wasn't sure of my surmise.'

'I believe you,' she said, 'for now, I think, you are bringing your eyes to look with greater care upon the truth. And what I am going to say is no less clear to the sight.'

'What is that?' I asked.

'Since we are right in thinking that God controls all things by the helm of goodness, and all things, as I have said, have a natural inclination towards the good, it can hardly be doubted, can it, that they are willingly governed and willingly obey the desires of him who controls them, as things that are in harmony and accord with their helmsman.'

'It is necessarily so, for it would hardly seem a happy government if it were like a yoke imposed upon unwilling necks instead of a willing acceptance of salvation.'

'There is nothing, therefore, which could preserve its own nature as well as go against God.'

'Nothing.'

'If it did try, it wouldn't make any progress against Him whom we have agreed to be, because of His happiness, supreme in power.'

'No, it would be completely powerless.'

'Is there anything, then, which might either wish to be or be able to withstand this supreme good?'

'I don't think so.'

'It is the supreme good, then, which mightily and sweetly orders all things.'

Then I said, 'The conclusion of this highest of arguments has made me very happy, and I am even more happy because of the words you used.[15] I am now ashamed of the stupidity of all my railing.'

'You have no doubt heard how in mythology the giants began attacking heaven,[16] and as was right, they, too, were kindly but firmly set to order. But would you like us to bring about a conflict of arguments? Perhaps from a collision of this kind some beautiful spark of truth might leap forth.'

'Whatever you decide,' I said.

'No one could doubt that God is omnipotent.'

'No one, at any rate, who is in his right mind would have any doubt about it.'

'But there is nothing that an omnipotent power could not do?'

'No.'

'Then, can God do evil?'

'No.'

'So that evil is nothing, since that is what He cannot do who can do anything.'

'You are playing with me, aren't you, by weaving a labyrinth of arguments from which I can't find the way out. At one moment you go in where you'll come out, and at another you come out where you went in. Or are you creating a wonderful circle of divine simplicity? Just now you began with happiness and said it was the highest good, and you said it was to be found in God. Then you began arguing that God Himself was also the supreme good and perfect happiness and added as a kind of bonus that no one could be happy unless he was also divine. You said that the very form of the good was identical with the substance of God and of happiness. And you taught us that unity itself was the same

15. When Boethius says, 'I am even more happy because of the words you used,' he is probably complimenting Philosophy for echoing the words of the Book of Wisdom 8, 1: 'Wisdom reacheth from one end to another mightily: and sweetly doth she order all things.' If this is so, it is an important indication of Boethius' attitude to faith and revelation: see Introduction, pp. 28 ff.

16. See Graves, op. cit., I, p. 131.

as the good, because all things had a natural inclination to it. Then you argued that God rules the universe by the helm of goodness, that all things obey willingly, and that evil is nothing. All of which you unfolded without the help of any external aid, but with one internal proof grafted upon another so that each drew its credibility from that which preceded.'

Then she replied, 'I am not mocking; through the favour of God whom we prayed to a moment ago, we have achieved the greatest of all things. The form of the divine substance is such that it does not spread out into outside things or take up into itself anything from them. As Parmenides says of it,

> like the mass of a sphere well-rounded in all ways[17]

it rotates the moving sphere of the universe while remaining itself unmoved. If we have been dealing with arguments not sought from without but within the bounds of the matter we have been discussing, there is no reason for you to be surprised. You have learnt on the authority of Plato that we must use language akin to the subject matter of our discourse.

> 'Happy the man whose eyes once could
> Perceive the shining fount of good;
> Happy he whose unchecked mind
> Could leave the chains of earth behind.
> 5 Once when Orpheus sad did mourn
> For his wife beyond death's bourn,
> His tearful melody begun
> Made the moveless trees to run,
> Made the rivers halt their flow,
> 10 Made the lion, hind's fell foe,
> Side by side with her to go,
> Made the hare accept the hound
> Subdued now by the music's sound.
> But his passions unrepressed
> 15 Burned more fiercely in his breast;
> Though his song all things subdued,

17. Plato, *Sophistes*, 244e.

It could not calm its master's mood.
Complaining of the gods above,
Down to hell he went for love.
20 There on sweetly sounding strings
Songs that soothe he plays and sings;
All the draughts once drawn of song
From the springs the Muses throng,
All the strength of helpless grief,
25 And of love which doubled grief,
Give their weight then to his weeping,
As he stands the lords beseeching
Of the underworld for grace.
The triform porter stands amazed,
30 By Orpheus' singing tamed and dazed;
The Furies who avenge men's sin,
Who at the guilty's terror grin,
Let tears of sorrow from them steal;
No longer does the turning wheel
35 Ixion's head send whirling round;
Old Tantalus upon the sound
Forgets the waters and his thirst,
And while the music is rehearsed
The vulture ceases flesh to shred.
40 At last the monarch of the dead
In tearful voice, "We yield," he said:
"Let him take with him his wife,
By song redeemed and brought to life.
But let him, too, this law obey,
45 Look not on her by the way
Until from night she reaches day."
But who to love can give a law?
Love unto itself is law.
Alas, close to the bounds of night
50 Orpheus backwards turned his sight
And, looking, lost and killed her there.
For you I sing the sad affair,
Whoever seek the upward way
To lift your mind into the day;

55   For who gives in and turns his eye
      Back to darkness from the sky,
      Loses while he looks below
      All that up with him may go.' [18]

18. Three main versions of the famous story of Orpheus and Eurydice were known to the Middle Ages, from Virgil (*Georgics*, IV, 453–527), Ovid (*Metamorphoses*, X–XI; cf. the Penguin Classics translation by Mary M. Innes, pp. 245 ff.), and Boethius, whose rendering here was perhaps the most influential of all, and was probably the version grafted on to the Celtic story pattern which lies behind the delightful Middle English poem *Sir Orfeo* (see *Medieval English Verse* by Brian Stone in the Penguin Classics, pp. 213 ff.). Of the population of Hades mentioned in the poem but not actually named, we have references to Cerberus, the three-headed guard dog of the Classical other world (line 29), Tityus, the giant whose liver was continuously devoured by vultures (line 39), and Pluto, the god of the lower world (line 40).

BOOK IV

I

PHILOSOPHY delivered this sweet and gentle song with dignity of countenance and gravity of expression. But I had still not forgotten the grief within me and I cut her short just as she was preparing to say something.

'You,' I said, 'who are my leader towards the true light, all that you have poured forth in speech up to now has been clearly both divine to contemplate and invincibly supported by your arguments. You have spoken of things I had forgotten because of the pain of what I had suffered, but before this they were not entirely unknown to me.

'But the greatest cause of my sadness is really this – the fact that in spite of a good helmsman to guide the world, evil can still exist and even pass unpunished. This fact alone you must surely think of considerable wonder. But there is something even more bewildering. When wickedness rules and flourishes, not only does virtue go unrewarded, it is even trodden underfoot by the wicked and punished in the place of crime. That this can happen in the realm of an omniscient and omnipotent God who wills only good, is beyond perplexity and complaint.'

'It would indeed be a matter of infinite wonder,' she said, 'it would be something more horrible than any outrage, if, as you reckon, in the well-ordered house of so great a father the worthless vessels were looked after at the expense of the precious ones, which grew filthy. But it is not so.

'If your recent conclusions may remain intact, you can learn from the Creator Himself since it is His realm we are speaking of, that the good are always strong and the wicked always humbled and weak. From Him, too, you can learn that sin never goes unpunished or virtue unrewarded, and that what happens to the good is always happy and that what happens to the bad always misfortune. There are many other considerations of this kind which, once your complaints have been stilled, will give you firm and solid strength.

'You have seen the shape of true happiness when I showed it to you just now, and you saw where it is to be found; and when we have run through all that I think we should clear out of the way beforehand, I will show you the path that will bring you back home. I will give your mind wings on which to lift itself; all disquiet shall be driven away and you will be able to return safely to your homeland. I will be your guide, your path and your conveyance.

'For I have swift and speedy wings
With which to mount the lofty skies,
And when thy mind has put them on
The earth below it will despise:
5 It mounts the air sublunary
And far behind the clouds it leaves;
It passes through the sphere of fire
Which from the ether heat receives,
Until it rises to the stars,
10 With Phoebus there to join its ways,
Or Saturn cold accompany
As soldier of his shining rays.
Wherever night is spangled bright
The orbit of a star it takes,
15 And when the orbit's path is done
The furthest heaven it forsakes.
It treads beneath the ether swift
Possessing now the holy light,
For here the King of kings holds sway,
20 The reins of all things holding tight,
Unmoving moves the chariot fast,
The lord of all things shining bright.
If there the pathway brings you back –
The path you lost and seek anew –

25 Then, "I remember," you will say,
    "My home, my source, my ending too."
    And if you choose to seek again
    The lightless earth which you have left,
    Dictators whom the people fear,
30 Will outcasts seem of home bereft.'[1]

II

Then I cried out in wonder at the magnitude of her promises. 'Not that I don't think you can do it,' I said. 'Only do not keep me waiting, now that you have whetted my appetite.'

'First then,' she said, 'that the good are always strong and that the wicked always bereft of all power, these are facts you will be able to see, the one being proved by the other. For since good and evil are opposites, the weakness of evil is shown by establishing the strength of good, and vice versa. So to strengthen your confidence in my teaching, I will proceed along both ways and prove my assertions doubly.

1. In this poem we have an account of the ascent of the soul to God, which must be understood in terms of the Boethian cosmos. The mind rises from the earth through the air to the sphere of the moon. At this point it leaves that part of the universe composed of the four elements, earth, air, water and fire; fire being the lightest of these has risen to just below the orbit of the moon where it forms its own sphere. Beyond the moon is the fifth element, the quintessence or ether. The soul continues to rise through the spheres of the stars (i.e. the wandering stars or planets as opposed to the fixed stars which are only reached in lines 13–14 after passing through the spheres of Mercury, Venus, Phoebus (= the sun), Mars, Jupiter and Saturn). Eventually the soul passes beyond the ether and reaches God, the source of the light emanating through the universe. The universe is turned inside out, as it were. God is seen as the centre of light. Earth as a place of darkness on the very edge of the universe. At birth the soul emanates or descends to the earth from God, and its ascent is an account of its return. See A. H. Armstrong, *An Introduction to Ancient Philosophy*, 3rd ed., London, 1957, Ch. 16, and F. Copleston, *A History of Philosophy*, Vol. I, part ii, Ch. 45 for the Plotinian version of this; and C. S. Lewis, *The Discarded Image*, Cambridge, 1964, Ch. 5 for the medieval version, and especially p. 116 for the 'inversion' of the universe from geocentric to theocentric. Cf. too the comparison of God to the still point in the middle of a series of concentric circles in IV, 6, a figure drawn from Plotinus. The metre was well-known in the middle ages and sprang to Chaucer's mind as he was carried aloft by the eagle in the *Hous of Fame*, ii. 972.

'Now, there are two things on which all the performance of human activity depends, will and power. If either of them is lacking, there is no activity that can be performed. In the absence of the will, a man is unwilling to do something and therefore does not undertake it; and in the absence of the power to do it, the will is useless. So that if you see someone who wants to get something which he cannot get, you can be sure that what he has been lacking is the power to get what he wanted.'

'It is obvious,' I said, 'and cannot be denied.'

'And if you see a man who has done what he wanted, you will hardly doubt that he had the power to do it, will you?'

'No.'

'Therefore, men's power or ability is to be judged by what they can do, and their weakness by what they can't do.'

'I agree.'

'Do you, then, remember how earlier in the argument we reached the conclusion that the instinctive direction of the human will, manifested through a variety of pursuits, was entirely towards happiness?'

'I remember that this was proved as well.'

'And you recall that happiness is the good itself and similarly that since they seek happiness, all men desire the good?'

'Not so much recall it, as hold it fixed in my mind.'

'So that without any difference of instinct all men, good and bad alike, strive to reach the good.'

'Yes, that follows.'

'But surely men become good by acquiring goodness?'

'Yes.'

'So that good men obtain what they are looking for?'

'It seems so.'

'But if the wicked obtained what they want – that is goodness – they could not be wicked?'

'No.'

'Since, then, both groups want goodness, and one obtains it

and the other doesn't, surely there can be no doubt of the power of the good and the weakness of the bad?'

'Anyone who does doubt it is no judge either of reality or the logic of argument.'

'Again,' she said, 'suppose there were two men who are set the same natural task, and one of them performs and completes it by natural action, while the other cannot manage the natural action, but uses another method contrary to nature, and does not actually complete the task but approximates to someone completing it; which would you say had the more power?'

'I can guess what you mean,' I said, 'but I would like to have it more clearly put.'

'You will not deny that the action of walking is natural and human, will you?'

'No.'

'And presumably you have no doubt that it is the natural function of the feet?'

'No, indeed.'

'If, then, one man is able to proceed on foot and goes walking, and another lacks the natural function of the feet and tries to walk on his hands, which may properly be considered the more able or powerful?'

'Ask me another! No one could doubt that the man who can do the natural action is more able than the one who can't.'

'Well, the supreme good is the goal of good men and bad alike, and the good seek it by means of a natural activity – the exercise of their virtues – while the bad strive to acquire the very same thing by means of their various desires, which isn't a natural method of obtaining the good. Or don't you agree?'

'Yes, for what follows is also obvious; from what I have already admitted it follows that the good are powerful and the bad weak.'

'You anticipate correctly. As the doctors like to think, it is a sign of a constitution strong and fighting back. But seeing you are so quick of understanding, I will pile the arguments on. Just think how great the weakness is that we see in wicked men; they can't even reach the goal to which almost by compulsion their natural inclination leads them. What if they were deserted by this great and almost invincible help, and nature ceased to show them the way?

'Think of the extent of the weakness impeding the wicked. It is not as if the prizes they failed to win were mere sports trophies. The quest in which they fail is the quest for the highest and most important of all things, and success is denied these wretched men in the very pursuit they toil at night and day to the exclusion of all else, the same pursuit in which the strength of the good stands out.

'If a man by walking could reach a point beyond which there was nowhere for him to go, you would consider him the champion at walking. In the same way you must judge the man who achieves the goal of all endeavour, beyond which there is nothing, to be supreme in power. The opposite of this is also true; those who do not gain it[2] are obviously lacking in all power.

'For I ask you, what is the cause of this flight from virtue to vice? If you say it is because they do not know what is good, I shall ask what greater weakness is there than the blindness of ignorance. And if you say that they know what they ought to seek for, but pleasure sends them chasing off the wrong way, this way too, they are weak through lack of self control because they cannot resist vice. And if you say they abandon

---

2. It is difficult to see exactly how the MS reading at this point (*idem scelesti idem viribus omnibus videantur esse deserti*) fits the context, and I therefore follow Bieler's suggestion that the original reading was something like *qui minime apprehendunt*; this, he suggests, was glossed *idē* (= *id est*) *scelesti*, which was later misinterpreted as *idem scelesti* and incorporated in the text to the exclusion of the true reading.

goodness and turn to vice knowingly and willingly, this way they not only cease to be powerful, but cease to be at all. Men who give up the common goal of all things that exist, thereby cease to exist themselves. Some may perhaps think it strange that we say that wicked men, who form the majority of men, do not exist; but that is how it is. I am not trying to deny the wickedness of the wicked; what I do deny is that their existence is absolute and complete existence. Just as you might call a corpse a dead man, but couldn't simply call it a man, so I would agree that the wicked are wicked, but could not agree that they have unqualified existence. A thing exists when it keeps its proper place and preserves its own nature. Anything which departs from this ceases to exist, because its existence depends on the preservation of its nature.

'To the objection that evil men do have power, I would say that this power of theirs comes from weakness rather than strength. For they would not have the power to do the evil they can if they could have retained the power of doing good. This power only makes it more clear that they can do nothing, for if, as we concluded a short time ago, evil i⁻ nothing, it is clear that since they can only do evil, the wicked can do nothing.'

'Obviously.'

'But I want you to understand the exact nature of the power we are talking about. A moment ago we decided that there is nothing with greater power than the supreme good.'

'That is so.'

'But supreme goodness cannot do evil.'

'No.'

'Now, no one thinks of human beings as omnipotent, do they?'

'Not unless they are mad.'

'But men can do evil?'

'I only wish they couldn't.'

'It is obvious, therefore, that since a power that can only do good is omnipotent, while human beings who can also do evil are not, these same human beings who can do evil are less powerful. In addition to this we have shown that all forms of power are to be included among those things worth pursuing, and that all these worthwhile objects of pursuit are related to the good as to a kind of aggregate of their nature. Now, the ability to commit a crime cannot be a form of goodness, and is therefore not worth pursuing. But all forms of power are worth seeking after, so that it is obvious that the ability to do evil is not a form of power.

'From all this the power of good men is obvious and, beyond all doubt, so is the weakness of bad men. And it is clear that what Plato said in the *Gorgias*[3] is true, namely that only the wise can achieve their desire, while the wicked busy themselves with what gives pleasure without being able to achieve their real objective. Their actions depend on the belief that they are going to obtain the good they desire through the things that give them pleasure. But they do not obtain it, because evil things cannot reach happiness.

> 'High kings you see sit loftily on thrones,
> In purple bright, by sober arms enhedged,
> With savage threat in passion's breathless rage;
> Once strip from pride their robes of empty show,
> And see within the straitening fetters worn:
> Here lust o'erthrows the heart with poisonous greed,
> Here like a wave wrath whips and bears off sense,
> Here captive sorrow sits or hope torments;
> Here in one heart so many tyrants rule,
> The king's own will's deposed, the enslaver slaved.'

III

'You can see, therefore, the filth in which crime wallows and the light in which goodness is resplendent. It is clear that good

3. 466b–481b.

123

deeds never lack reward, or crimes their appropriate punishment. The proper way of looking at it is to regard the goal of every action as its reward, just as the prize for running in the stadium is the wreath of laurels for which the race is run. Now, we have shown that happiness is the very same good which motivates all activity; so that goodness itself is set as a kind of common reward of human activity. But goodness cannot be removed from those who are good; therefore, goodness never fails to receive its appropriate reward. So despite all the raging of the wicked, the wise man's crown of laurels will never fall from him or wither away. The wickedness of others can never wrest their individual glory from the good. If it was a borrowed glory that we prided ourselves upon, other people including the very one who conferred it on us could take it away; but since the glory is conferred on each one by his own goodness he will only lose his reward when he stops being good.

'Finally since every reward is desired because it is believed to be good, no one will consider a man endowed with goodness to be without reward. But what kind of reward? The greatest and most beautiful of all. Think again of that corollary I emphasized to you a short time ago, and consider it this way. Goodness is happiness, and therefore it is obvious that all good men obtain happiness in virtue of their being good. But we agree that those who attain happiness are divine. The reward of the good, then, a reward that can never be decreased, that no one's power can diminish, and no one's wickedness darken, is to become gods. This being so, no wise man can be in any doubt of the inevitability of the punishment of the wicked. Like good and evil, reward and punishment are opposites. The reward we see due to the good must be balanced by a corresponding punishment of the wicked. Therefore, just as goodness is its own reward, so the punishment of the wicked is their very wickedness. Now, no one who suffers a punishment doubts that he suffers something

reward for good = become gods

evil. So, if they are willing to examine themselves, I do not think men can consider themselves immune from punishment when they suffer the worst evil of all: evil is not so much an infliction as a deep set infection.

'Again, think of the punishment that dogs the wicked from the opposite point of view of the good. A short while ago you learned that all that exists is in a state of unity and that goodness itself is unity; from which it follows that we must see everything that exists as good. This means that anything which turns away from goodness ceases to exist, and thus that the wicked cease to be what they once were. That they used to be human is shown by the human appearance of their body which still remains. So it was by falling into wickedness that they also lost their human nature. Now, since only goodness can raise a man above the level of human kind, it follows that it is proper that wickedness thrusts down to a level below mankind those whom it has dethroned from the condition of being human.

'The result is that you cannot think of anyone as human whom you see transformed by wickedness. You could say that someone who robs with violence and burns with greed is like a wolf. A wild and restless man who is for ever exercising his tongue in lawsuits could be compared to a dog yapping. A man whose habit is to lie hidden in an ambush and steal by trapping people would be likened to a fox. A man of quick temper has only to roar to gain the reputation of a lion-heart. The timid coward who is terrified when there is nothing to fear is thought to be like the hind. The man who is lazy, dull and stupid, lives an ass's life. A man of whimsy and fickleness who is for ever changing his interests is just like a bird. And a man wallowing in foul and impure lusts is occupied by the filthy pleasures of a sow. So what happens is that when a man abandons goodness and ceases to be human, being unable to rise to a divine condition, he sinks to the level of being an animal.

'The sails of the lord of Ithaca[4]
And his wandering sea-borne ships
Were blown from the East to the island
Where a beautiful goddess lives,
Circe, daughter of the sun.
For her new-come guests she mixes
Cups she has touched with a spell;
In various shapes they are changed
By her hands in herb-lore skilled.
One takes the form of a boar,
And one an African lion
Grows in fang and claw.
Another becomes a wolf,
Can't weep, can only howl;
And here like an Indian tiger
One gently pads around.
Perils surround lord Odysseus,
But the winged Arcadian god
Takes pity on his plight,
Saves him from Circe's curse.
Odysseus' crew have drunk
The evil powered draughts,
And leave the bread men eat
To seek as pigs for husks:
Nothing is left intact,
Their voice and body changed;
Only the mind remains
To mourn their monstrous plight.
But Circe's hand was weak,
Her herbs were powerless;
They changed the body's limbs
But could not change the heart;
Safe in a secret fastness
The strength of man lies hid.

4. The lord of Ithaca is, of course, Odysseus, the story of whose long
delayed homecoming from the siege of Troy forms the subject matter of
Homer's *Odyssey*. His adventure on the island of Circe and his deliverance
by Hermes – the winged Arcadian god – who gave him the scented white
flower Moly as a charm against her magic are related in book 10.

Those poisons, though, are stronger,
Which creeping deep within,
Dethrone a man's true self:
They do not harm the body,
But cruelly wound the mind.'

IV

Then I said, 'I agree, and I see the justice of saying that though they retain the outward appearance of the human body, wicked people change into animals with regard to their state of mind. But I could have wished that no freedom was allowed to the fury of cruel and wicked-minded men to bring destruction on the good.'

'It's not a question of freedom,' she said, 'as I will show at the appropriate point. But supposing the freedom they are believed to enjoy were removed, it would to a large extent mean relieving criminals of their punishment. It may seem incredible to some, but it must be the case that the wicked are less happy if they achieve their desires than if they are unable to do what they want. For, if desiring something wicked brings misery, greater misery is brought by having had the power to do it, without which the unhappy desire would go unfulfilled. So, since each stage has its own degree of misery, if you see people with the desire to do something wicked, the power to do it and the achievement, they must necessarily suffer a triple degree of misfortune.'

'Yes, I agree: but I hope very much that they will soon be released from this misfortune by losing the power to do evil.'

'They will be released sooner than perhaps you would wish or they themselves expect. For in the very short space of a human life, nothing can be so late in coming as to seem to the mind long to wait for, especially as it is immortal. Their great hope and their ambitious blue-print of crime is often destroyed by a sudden and unexpected end, which does at least impose a limit on their misery. For if wickedness is the cause of their misery, it follows that their wickedness makes them the more wretched the longer it lasts. If death did not at last end their evil, I would count them the unhappiest of men. For obviously if our conclusions about the misfortune of wickedness are true, any misery which is agreed to be everlasting is infinite.'

'It is a strange thing to conclude and hard to accept, but I do see that it fits in with our previous admissions.'

'You are right,' she said, 'but if someone thinks a particular conclusion hard to accept, he ought to show either that some false assumption has preceded it or that the way the arguments have been marshalled does not necessarily produce the conclusion. Otherwise, provided he agrees to what has preceded, there is absolutely no ground for arguing about the conclusion. What I am going to say may also seem no less strange, but it is an equally necessary conclusion from our assumptions.'

'What is it?' I asked.

'That the wicked are happier if they suffer punishment than if they are unrestrained by any just retribution. And I do not have in mind what you may think, namely that wickedness is corrected by punishment and returned to the path of right by the fear of punishment, and is also an example to others to avoid punishable actions. No, I think there is another way in which the wicked are more unhappy if they go unpunished, apart from any consideration of the corrective effect of punishment or its value as a deterrent to others.'

'What other way is there?'

'Well, we have agreed, haven't we, that the good men are happy and the bad unhappy?'

'Yes.'

'Now, if someone's misery is offset by something good, he is happier than someone else whose misery is pure and undiluted by any admixture of good, isn't he?'

'So it seems.'

'What if that same unhappy person, who has no share of

anything good, should receive some further evil in addition
to those that have caused his unhappiness, he would have to
be considered far more unhappy, wouldn't he, than the one
whose misfortune is lessened by a share of good?'

'Of course.'

'Now, obviously the punishment of the wicked is just, and
their escape from punishment unjust.'

'No one would deny that.'

'And no one will deny, too, that what is just is good, and on
the other hand, what is unjust is bad.'

I agreed it was obvious.

'So when the wicked receive punishment they receive
something good, the punishment itself, which is good,
because of its justice; but when they go unpunished they
acquire some extra evil in actually going scot free, which you
have agreed is bad, because of its injustice.'

'I cannot deny it.'

'So the wicked are much more unhappy when they are
unjustly allowed to go scot free, than when a just punishment
is imposed upon them.'

'It is the logical outcome of our previous conclusion. But,
I ask you, don't you leave any punishment of the soul until
after the death of the body?'

'There is, indeed, great punishment then, sometimes
exacted with penal severity, sometimes, I think, with purifying
mercy; but it is not my intention to discuss it now.

'We have followed the argument as far as we have for you
to see that what you thought of as the entirely undeserved
power of the wicked is no power at all. I wanted you to see
that those whose freedom from punishment you were
complaining of do not at all escape paying for their wickedness. That freedom of theirs for whose speedy end you were
praying doesn't last long and will be the more miserable the
longer it continues. It will be most miserable of all if it is
endless. And lastly, the wicked are more wretched when

unjustly absolved from punishment than when they receive a just retribution. The logical conclusion of this is that they are burdened with heavier punishment precisely when they are believed to escape it.'

Then I said, 'When I consider your arguments, I think nothing more true could be spoken. But when I turn to the opinions of ordinary men, few would even grant you a hearing, let alone believe you.'

'It is true,' she said. 'Their eyes are used to the dark and they cannot raise them to the shining light of truth. They are like birds whose sight is sharpened by night and blinded by day. So long as they look only at their own desires and not the order of creation, they think of freedom to commit crimes and the absence of punishment as happy things. But let us see what is decreed by everlasting law: if you have turned your mind to higher things, there is no need of a judge to award a prize; it is you yourself who have brought yourself to a more excellent state: but if you have directed your zeal towards lower things, do not look for punishment from without; it is you yourself who have plunged yourself into the worse condition – just as if you look by turns at the sky and the dirt of the earth, and everything else disappears and you seem at one moment to be in the mud and at the next moment among the stars, just by the action of looking. But ordinary people do not see such things.

'Well, are we to join these people whom we have shown to be like animals? What about the case of a man who completely lost his sight and even forgot he had ever had it and thought that he had everything that belonged to human perfection; would we who had sight think the same as the blind man?

'And there is something else equally well founded on a firm base of argument which they will not agree with, namely that those who commit an injustice are more unhappy than those who suffer it.'

130

'I would like to hear the argument.'

'Well, I presume you do not deny that every wicked man deserves punishment?'

'No.'

'And it is abundantly clear that the wicked are unhappy?'

'Yes.'

'Therefore you would not doubt the unhappiness of those who deserve punishment?'

'No.'

'Suppose, then, you were sitting in judgment in the law courts; on whom would you decide to pass sentence, the man who had committed the wrong, or the man who had suffered it?'

'I have no hesitation in saying I would satisfy the one who had suffered at the expense of the one who had done it.'

'So you would think the perpetrator of the injury more wretched than the victim?'

'It follows.'

'For this and other reasons based on the fact that by its own nature badness makes men wretched, it is clear that when someone is done an injury, the misery belongs not to the victim but to the perpetrator.[5]

'But the court orators of today take the opposite course; they try to excite the sympathy of the court for those who have suffered some grievous and painful injury, although a juster sympathy is more due to those who are guilty. They ought to be brought to justice not by a prosecution counsel with an air of outrage, but by a prosecution kind and sympathetic, like sick men being brought to the doctor, so that their guilt could be cut back by punishment like a malignant growth. In this way the work of the defence counsel would either completely come to a standstill, or, if they chose to benefit mankind, they would turn to the job of accusation.

5. Bieler suggests that at this point we have lost a reply from Boethius. The reply would be 'Yes, it is clear', or something like it.

And the wicked themselves, if through some crack they were allowed a glimpse of the virtue they had abandoned, if they could see themselves about to lay aside the filth of vice through the pains of punishment, they would no longer consider them to be pains because of the compensation of acquiring goodness, and they would refuse the services of defence counsels and give themselves up wholly to their accusers and judges.

'This is why among wise men there is no place at all left for hatred. For no one except the greatest of fools would hate good men. And there is no reason at all for hating the bad. For just as weakness is a disease of the body, so wickedness is a disease of the mind. And if this is so, since we think of people who are sick in body as deserving sympathy rather than hatred, much more so do they deserve pity rather than blame who suffer an evil more severe than any physical illness.

'What pleasure do men find in passions high
And tempting fate with suicidal hand?
If they seek death, unbid he'll soon draw nigh,
Giving his steeds free rein to speed him forth.
Man is the prey of lion fangs and snake,
Of tiger, bear and boar; is man the prey
Of man as well? Why does he battles make
And long to perish by another's blade?
Because his manners differ – just for this?
No just cause there for blood and savageness.
You want desert no due reward to miss?
Then love the good, show pity for the bad.'

V

Then I said, 'Yes, I can see there is a kind of happiness and misery which are inseparable from the very actions of good and bad men. But I believe that there is both good and bad in the actual fortune of ordinary people. No wise man prefers being in exile, being poor and disgraced to being rich, respected, and powerful, and to remaining at home and flourishing in his own city. For this is the way that wisdom is more clearly and obviously seen to be operating, when somehow or other the happiness of their rulers is communicated to the people they come into contact with, especially if prison and death and all the other sufferings the law imposes by way of punishment are reserved for the wicked citizens for whom they were intended. Why this is all turned upside down, why good men are oppressed by punishments reserved for crime and bad men can snatch the rewards that belong to virtue surprises me very much, and I would like to know from you the reason for this very unjust confusion. I would be less surprised if I could believe that the confusion of things is due to the fortuitous operations of chance. But my wonder is only increased by the knowledge that the ruling power of the universe is God. Sometimes He is pleasant to the good and unpleasant to the bad, and other times He grants the bad their wishes and denies the good. But since He often varies between these two alternatives, what grounds are there for distinguishing between God and the haphazards of chance?'

'It is not surprising,' she said, 'if ignorance of the principle of its order makes people think a thing is unplanned and chaotic. But even if you don't know the reason behind the great plan of the universe, there is no need for you to doubt that a good power rules the world and that everything happens aright.

'If you knew not the stars of Arcturus
 Sail near the highest pole of heaven, or why
 The Waggoner is late to take his wain
 And late to dip his flames into the sea
 Although his rising comes again with haste,
 The law observed in heaven would leave you dazed.
 And let the full moon's gleaming horns grow pale
 As night extends his bounds across her disc;
 Let Phoebe dimmed the confused stars reveal
 Which just before her shining light had masked;

Whole nations by the common error moved
Rain frequent blows on pots and pans of brass.[6]
Yet no one wonders when the north west wind
Sweeps in the roaring waves to beat the shore,
Or when the frozen mass of hard-packed snow
Dissolves before the sun's aestival heat.
The causes in this case are clear to view,
But hidden cause confounds the human heart,
Perplexed by things that rarely come to pass,
For unexpected things the people dread.
Then let the clouds of ignorance give way
And these events will no more wondrous seem.'

VI

'It is so,' I said. 'But since it is part of your task to unravel the causes of matters that lie hidden and to unfold reasons veiled in darkness, and since I am very much disturbed by this strange phenomenon, I do beg you to tell me your teaching on this point.'

She paused and smiled a moment before answering.

'You are urging me to the greatest of all questions, a question that can never be exhausted. The subject is of such a kind that when one doubt has been removed, countless others spring up in its place, like the Hydra's heads. The only way to check them is with a really lively intellectual fire. The usual subjects of inquiry concern the oneness of providence, the course of fate, the haphazard nature of the random events of chance, divine knowledge and predestination, and the freedom of the will; you can see for yourself how difficult they are.

'However, as a knowledge of these things, too, is a part of

6. G. G. Ramsay comments on Satire VI lines 442–3 in the Loeb edition of Juvenal: 'Eclipses of the moon were supposed by the ignorant to be due to the incantations of witches. To prevent these from being heard, and so to ward off the evil events portended by the eclipse, it was the custom to create a din by the clashing of bells, horns, trumpets, etc.'

your treatment, we will try to determine something, in spite of the narrow limits in which we are imprisoned by time. And if the enchantments of song delight you, you will have to postpone your pleasure a little while I weave together the close-knit arguments in their proper order.'

'Whatever you wish,' I said.

Then, as if she were starting a fresh argument, she spoke as follows.

'The generation of all things, the whole progress of things subject to change and whatever moves in any way, receive their causes, their due order and their form from the unchanging mind of God. In the high citadel of its oneness, the mind of God has set up a plan for the multitude of events. When this plan is thought of as in the purity of God's understanding, it is called Providence, and when it is thought of with reference to all things, whose motion and order it controls, it is called by the name the ancients gave it, Fate. If anyone will examine their meaning, it will soon be clear to him that these two aspects are different. Providence is the divine reason itself. It is set at the head of all things and disposes all things. Fate, on the other hand, is the planned order inherent in things subject to change through the medium of which Providence binds everything in its own allotted place. Providence includes all things at the same time, however diverse or infinite, while Fate controls the motion of different individual things in different places and in different times. So this unfolding of the plan in time when brought together as a unified whole in the foresight of God's mind is Providence; and the same unified whole when dissolved and unfolded in the course of time is Fate.

'They are different, but the one depends on the other. The order of Fate is derived from the simplicity of Providence. A craftsman anticipates in his mind the plan of the thing he is going to make, and then sets in motion the execution of the work and carries out in time the construction of what he has seen all at one moment present to his mind's eye. In the same

way God in his Providence constructs a single fixed plan of
all that is to happen, while it is by means of Fate that all that
He has planned is realized in its many individual details in the
course of time. So, whether the work of Fate is done with the
help of divine spirits of Providence, or whether the chain of
Fate is woven by the soul of the universe, or by the obedience
of all nature, by the celestial motions of the stars, or by the
power of the angels, by the various skills of other spirits, or
by some of these, or by all of them, one thing is certainly
clear: the simple and unchanging plan of events is Providence,
and Fate is the ever-changing web, the disposition in and
through time of all the events which God has planned in His
simplicity.

'Everything, therefore, which comes under Fate, is also
subject to Providence, to which Fate itself is subject, but
certain things which come under Providence are above the
chain of Fate. These are things which rise above the order of
change ruled over by Fate in virtue of the stability of their
position close to the supreme Godhead. Imagine a set of
revolving concentric circles. The inmost one comes closest to
the simplicity of the centre, while forming itself a kind of
centre for those set outside it to revolve round. The circle
furthest out rotates through a wider orbit and the greater its
distance from the indivisible centre point, the greater the space
it spreads through. Anything that joins itself to the middle
circle is brought close to simplicity, and no longer spreads out
widely. In the same way whatever moves any distance from
the primary intelligence becomes enmeshed in ever stronger
chains of Fate, and everything is the freer from Fate the
closer it seeks the centre of things. And if it cleaves to the
steadfast mind of God, it is free from movement and so
escapes the necessity imposed by Fate. The relationship
between the ever-changing course of Fate and the stable
simplicity of Providence is like that between reasoning and
understanding, between that which is coming into being and

that which is, between time and eternity, or between the moving circle and the still point in the middle.

'The course of Fate moves the sky and the stars, governs the relationship between the elements and transforms them through reciprocal variations; it renews all things as they come to birth and die away by like generations of offspring and seed. It holds sway, too, over the acts and fortunes of men through the indissoluble chain of causes; and since it takes its origins from unchanging Providence, it follows that these causes, too, are unchanging. For the best way of controlling the universe is if the simplicity immanent in the divine mind produces an unchanging order of causes to govern by its own incommutability everything that is subject to change, and which will otherwise fluctuate at random.

'It is because you men are in no position to contemplate this order that everything seems confused and upset. But it is no less true that everything has its own position which directs it towards the good and so governs it. There is nothing that can happen because of evil or because engineered by the wicked themselves, and they, as we have most amply demonstrated, are deflected from their search for the good by mistake and error, while the order which issues from the supreme good at the centre of the universe cannot deflect anyone from his beginning.

'No doubt your objection will be that it is impossible for there to be a more unjust confusion than when the fortunes of good men and bad alike continually vary between adversity and prosperity. And I shall ask you if men have such soundness of mind as to be infallible in their judgement of who is good and who is bad. No, human judgements clash in this matter, and some people think the same men deserve reward as others think worthy of punishment.

'Supposing, however, we grant that someone may be able to judge between good and bad, it will hardly enable him to see the inner hidden temperament, to borrow a term from physics,[7] of men's minds. Indeed, your surprise is like that of a man who does not know why in the case of healthy bodies sweet things agree with some and bitter things with others, or why some sick people are helped by gentle remedies, others by sharp ones. But it is no surprise to the doctor who knows the difference between the manner and temper of health and of sickness. Now, we know that in the case of the mind health means goodness and sickness means wickedness. And that the protector of the good and scourge of the wicked is none other than God, the mind's guide and physician. He looks out from the watch-tower of Providence, sees what suits each person, and applies to him whatever He knows is suitable. This, then, is the outstanding wonder of the order of fate; a knowing God acts and ignorant men look on with wonder at his actions.

'Let us glance at a few facts concerning God's profundity, such as human reason can grasp. In the case of someone you consider a model and a great defender of justice, omniscient Providence thinks otherwise. A member of my own household, the poet Lucan, has reminded us in the first book of his *Pharsalia* how in the struggle between Caesar and Pompey the winning cause pleased the Gods, but the losing cause pleased Cato, although he was a model of virtue.[8] Whenever, therefore, you see something happen here different from your expectation, due order is preserved by events, but there is confusion and error in your thinking.

'But let us suppose that there was someone of such moral goodness that in his case the judgement of man and God

7. Strictly speaking the English term *temperament* (as well as the terms *temper* and *temperature*) is a borrowing from medieval physics in which all three referred to a mixture or combination of the four elements earth, air, fire, and water.

8. *Pharsalia*, I. 128. See the Penguin translation, p. 29. M. Porcius Cato (95–46 B.C.) was well known for his rigid morality. He joined Pompey in the civil war against Caesar, and committed suicide rather than suffer capture after Caesar's victory in the battle of Thapsus. Lucan characterizes Cato as the personification of Godlike virtue; see especially *Pharsalia*, book IX.

coincided; he will still be weak in strength of mind. Should adversity befall him, he will perhaps give up practising the innocence which could not ensure his good fortune. And so a wise direction spares the man whom adversity might affect for the worse, to avoid distressing someone who is not fit for it. Another man may be perfect in every virtue, holy and very close to God: Providence judges that it would be outrageous for him to meet with any adversity to such an extent that he is not even allowed to be upset by bodily illness. As was said by someone more excellent than me:[9]

> The body of the holy one was built by heaven.

'Often it happens that supreme power is given to good men so that the exuberance of wickedness may be checked. Others receive a mixture of good and bad fortune according to their quality of mind. Providence stings some people to avoid giving them happiness for too long, and others she allows to be vexed by hard fortune to strengthen their virtues of mind by the use and exercise of patience. Some people are excessively afraid of suffering for which they actually have the endurance; others are full of scorn for suffering they cannot in fact bear. Both kinds she brings to self-discovery through hardship. Some men at the price of a glorious death have won a fame that generations will venerate; some indomitable in the face of punishment have given others an example that evil cannot defeat virtue. There is no doubt that it is right that these things happen, that they are planned and that they are suited to those to whom they actually happen.

'The fact, too, that the wicked have their ups and downs of fortune is due to the same causes. When they suffer, no one is surprised, because everyone considers they deserve ill; and their punishments both deter others from crime and correct those on whom they are inflicted. And when they prosper, it is a powerful argument to good men about the kind of

9. Source unknown.

judgement they should make of such happiness as they often see wait upon the wicked. And here there is something else I believe to be planned. There is perhaps someone of such a headstrong and impulsive nature that poverty could the more easily provoke him to crime. His sickness is relieved by Providence with a dose of wealth as a remedy. Another man may see his conscience blotched with the wickedness of his deeds and compare his desert with the fortune he enjoys. Perhaps he will begin to fear the hardness of losing all the things whose enjoyment is so pleasant, and therefore change his ways and abandon wickedness in the fear of losing happiness. Others have been thrown headlong into well deserved disaster by using their happiness unworthily: and some were granted the right to punish in order that they might be a source of trial for the good and of punishment for the bad. For just as there is no agreement between good men and bad men, so even the bad cannot agree amongst themselves. It could scarcely be otherwise when with his own vices tearing his conscience in shreds each one is at loggerheads with himself, and they often do things which they later see should never have been done.

'And so sovereign Providence has often produced a remarkable effect – evil men making other evil men good. For some, when they think they suffer injustice at the hands of the worst of men, burn with hatred for evil men, and being eager to be different from those they hate, have reformed and become virtuous. It is only the power of God to which evils may also be good, when by their proper use He elicits some good result. For a certain order embraces all things, and anything which departs from the order planned and assigned to it, only falls back into order, albeit a different order, so as not to allow anything to chance in the realm of Providence.

'But as the *Iliad* puts it,

'Tis hard for me to speak as though a God.[10]

10. *Iliad*, 12, 176.

And it is not allowed to man to comprehend in thought all the ways of the divine work or expound them in speech. Let it be enough that we have seen that God, the author of all natures, orders all things and directs them towards goodness. He is quick to hold all that He has created in His own image, and by means of the chain of necessity presided over by Fate banishes all evil from the bounds of His commonwealth. Evil is thought to abound on earth. But if you could see the plan of Providence, you would not think there was evil anywhere. But I see that you have long been bowed down by the weight of this question. You are worn out by the prolixity of the reasoning and have been looking forward to the sweetness of song. So take a draught that will refresh you and make you able to apply your thoughts more closely to further matters.

> 'If you desire to see and understand
> In purity of mind the laws of God,
> Your sight must on the highest point of heaven rest
> Where through the lawful covenant of things
> The wandering stars preserve their ancient peace:
> The sun forth driven by his glittering flames
> Stays not the orbit of the gelid moon;
> Nor does the Bear who in the highest pole
> Of heaven drives her swiftly-turning course
> Which never to the western sea descends
> Desire to follow other stars that set,
> And merge her fire beneath the Atlantic deep:
> By equal intervals of time each day
> The Evening Star foretells the evening dusk
> And comes again as Morning Star at dawn.
> So everlasting courses are remade
> By mutual love and war's disunion
> Is banished from the shores of heaven above.
> This concord governs all the elements
> With equal measures, that the power of wet
> Will yield by turns unto the hostile dry,

And cold will join in amity with hot;
The pendant fire will surge into the air,
And massive weight of earth will sink below.
And for these reasons when the spring grows warm
The flower-bearing year will breathe sweet scent,
In summer torrid days will dry the corn,
Ripe autumn will return with fruit endowed,
And falling rains will moisten wintry days.
This mixture brings to birth and nourishes
All things which breathe the breath of life on earth;
This mixture seizes, hides, and bears away
All things submerged in death's finality.
Meanwhile there sits on high the Lord of things,
Who rules and guides the reins of all that's made,
Their king and lord, their fount and origin,
Their law and judge of what is right and due.
All things that He with motion stirs to go
He holds and when they wander brings them back;
Unless He call them home to their true path,
And force them back their orbits to perfect,
Those things which stable order now protects,
Divorced from their true source would fall apart.
This is the love of which all things partake,
The end of good their chosen goal and close:
No other way can they expect to last,
Unless with love for love repaid they turn
And seek again the cause that gave them birth.'

VII

'Do you now see what is the consequence of all that we
have said?'
'No, what is it?'
'All fortune is certainly good.'
'How can that be?'
'Listen. All fortune whether pleasant or adverse is meant
either to reward or discipline the good or to punish or correct

the bad. We agree, therefore, on the justice or usefulness of fortune, and so all fortune is good.'

'Your argument is very true, and if I were thinking of the Providence you taught me about just now and of Fate, your opinion would be firmly founded. But let us please include it among those opinions we some time ago called inconceivable.'

'Why so?' she asked.

'Because it is a common expression, frequently used by some, that people have bad fortune.'

'Your wish, then, is that we should draw closer to everyday language to avoid the appearance of having moved too far from common usage?'

'Yes, please.'

'Well, you think of something that is useful as being good, don't you?'

'Yes.'

'Now, such fortune as either disciplines or corrects is useful, isn't it?'

'Yes.'

'And so good?'

'Yes.'

'Now this kind of fortune is that of men who are either already on the path of virtue when they battle with adversity, or who turn to the path of virtue after quitting evil.'

'It is so.'

'What about the pleasant fortune, then, that is given to good men as a reward? People don't say this is bad, do they?'

'No. They hold it to be extremely good, as it is.'

'Then what about the last kind of fortune, which is adverse and curbs the bad with due punishment; do people think this is good?'

'No, they don't; they consider it to be the most miserable thing that can be imagined.'

'Take care that in following popular opinions we haven't produced something really inconceivable!'

'What do you mean?'

'Well, the result of all that we have agreed is that whatever the fortune of those who are in possession of virtue (whether that possession is perfect, still growing or only incipient), it is good, while the fortune of all those who rest in wickedness is utterly bad.'

'This is true, even if no one would dare to admit it.'

'So a wise man ought no more to take it ill when he clashes with fortune than a brave man ought to be upset by the sound of battle. For both of them their very distress is an opportunity, for the one to gain glory and the other to strengthen his wisdom. This is why virtue gets its name, because it is firm in strength and unconquered by adversity.[11]

'For you who are set on the path of increasing virtue have not come so far only to abandon yourself to delights or languish in pleasure. You are engaged in a bitter but spirited struggle against fortune of every kind, to avoid falling victim to her when she is adverse or being corrupted by her when she is favourable. Hold to the middle way with unshakeable strength. Whatever falls short or goes beyond, despises happiness but receives no reward for its toil. It is in your own hands what fortune you wish to shape for yourself, for the only function of adversity apart from discipline and correction, is punishment.

'For twice five years did Agamemnon war,
    The ruthless son of Atreus, till at Troy
    He vengeance took for wedlock set at naught;
    The same who when he wished the Grecian fleet
5   To sail, with blood did purchase favouring winds,
    Put off the father, and turned dismal priest

11. Boethius' pun cannot be imitated in English: following Varro and Cicero, he plays on the similarity between the Latin words *virtus*, virtue, and *vires*, strength.

To maculate a wretched daughter's throat.[12]
   Odysseus wept for his companions lost
When Polyphemus in his cavern vast
10 Lay back and plunged them in his monstrous crop;
The Cyclops, eyeless, blinded, raged with pain
And paid the price of joy with woeful tears.[13]
   Great Hercules is famous for his toils;
At Pholoë he tamed the Centaurs proud;
15 At Nemea he won the lion's pelt;
His arrows pierced the birds of Stymphalus,
And from beneath the dragon's gaze he snatched
The golden fruit of the Hesperides.
The captured Cerberus he led in chains,
20 And when he won the mares of Diomede
He served their master's flesh for them to eat.
He burnt the Hydra and its poison fell,
And dealt a shameful wound to Acheloüs
Who hid beneath his banks his face disgraced.
25 In Lybia he laid Antaeus low;
And Cacus satisfied Evander's wrath.
Those shoulders which the heavens were to press,
With froth the Erymanthian boar defiled.
His final labour was to hold the skies
30 On neck unbent, and for this latest feat[14]
He earned a place in heaven as his reward.

12. ll.1–7. The cause of the Trojan war here described was the elopement by the Trojan prince, Paris, with Helen, the wife of Agamemnon's brother Menelaus. Agamemnon became commander-in-chief of the Greek expedition to recover Helen, and was forced to sacrifice his daughter, Iphigeneia, to the Goddess Artemis, whom he had offended, before the fleet could obtain a fair wind for the voyage to Troy. After ten years of seige Troy was eventually sacked by the Greeks.

13. ll.8–12. Another member of the Greek forces was Odysseus. One of his adventures on the homeward journey from Troy concerned the one-eyed Cyclops, Polyphemus, who captured Odysseus and his men in his cave and began to eat them. Polyphemus became drunk, and while he slept Odysseus and his men heated a stave and put out his eye. Thus blinded, the giant was unable to prevent their escape. See the *Odyssey*, book 9.

14. ll.13–31. One of the most famous subjects of Greek myth is the hero Hercules, a man of outstanding strength. He was set a series of twelve labours

Go now, ye strong, where the exalted way
Of great example leads. Why hang you back?
Why turn away? Once earth has been surpassed
It gives the stars.'

---

by Eurystheus, some of which Boethius alludes to here, although not in their usual order. The labours mentioned are:

1. The fight with the Nemean lion whose skin Eurystheus ordered Hercules to bring him (l.15).

2. The fight against the Hydra, a monster with nine heads; each time Hercules struck off one of the heads, two new ones grew in its place. It could only be destroyed by fire (l.22).

4. The destruction of the Erymanthian boar (l.28) in the course of which Hercules came to the centaur Pholus – a creature half horse and half man – who entertained Hercules with a cask of wine, the delicious flavour of which so attracted all the other centaurs that they laid siege to Pholus' cave. Eventually Hercules overcame them (l.14).

6. The destruction of the Stymphalian birds, who lived on human flesh; Eurystheus ordered Hercules to drive them away from lake Stymphalus (l.16).

8. The capture of the man-eating mares kept by Diomedes, king of the Bistones in Thrace. Eurystheus ordered Hercules to bring them to him and when he had captured them and subdued the Bistones, Hercules fed the mares on the flesh of Diomedes which deprived them of their fierceness (ll.20–21).

10. The capture of the oxen of Geryon, reputedly the strongest man alive. On the return journey after the successful accomplishment of this task Hercules met king Evander; while Hercules was resting the three-headed shepherd Cacus stole some of the finest of the cattle and hid them in his cave; Cacus paid for his crime with his life (l.26).

11. The fetching of the golden apples of the Hesperides, guarded by the dragon on Mount Atlas (ll.17–18). After killing the dragon Hercules asked Atlas to fetch the apples, and while he did so, Hercules took the weight of heaven upon his own shoulders (ll.27 and 29–30). On his return from this labour, Hercules was forced into a wrestling match with Antaeus, king of Lybia, whom he eventually overcame (l.25).

12. The bringing of Cerberus, the monstrous dog who guarded the entrance to Hades, from the lower world (l.19).

On another occasion Hercules fought with a fellow suitor for the hand of Deianeira; the rival suitor, Achelous, was really a river-god, but could also take the form of a bull. In this form Hercules felled him and broke off one of his horns; to conceal the shameful wound the river-god went and hid his face in the river bank (ll.23–4).

On his death the immortal part of Hercules was taken up into heaven and made a god (l.31).

BOOK V

I

SHE stopped speaking and was about to move on to deal with certain other topics when I broke in.

'Your exhortation is very fitting and appropriate to one of your authority. But you said just now that the question of Providence was bound up with many others, and I want to put it to the test. I want to know whether you think there is such a thing as chance, and what it is.'

'The promise I made is a debt I owe you and I am ready to repay it,' she said, 'and to open the way for you to regain your true home. But useful as it is to know about these other matters, they are somewhat aside from our proposed path, and I am afraid you may be so worn out by digressions that you will be unable to complete the journey.'

'Don't worry about that,' I rejoined. 'It will be as good as a rest to be able to see the things which most delight me. At the same time, since your argument has stood firm on every side and its trustworthiness has remained undoubted, there need be no doubt about what comes next.'

'I will obey your wish,' she said, and began at once as follows.

'If chance is defined as an event produced by random motion without any causal nexus, I would say that there is no such thing as chance, and that apart from signifying the subject matter of our discussion it is a completely meaningless word. If God imposes order upon all things, there is no opportunity for random events. It is a true maxim that nothing comes out of nothing. None of the ancients denied it, although they used it as an axiom of their natural philosophy with special reference to material objects, not efficient causes. If something does happen for no cause, it obviously arises out of nothing;

but if this is impossible, it is impossible, too, for there to be chance of the kind we have just defined.'

'Well, then,' I asked, 'isn't there anything which can properly be called chance or accidental? Isn't there something for which these words are appropriate, even though ordinary people don't recognize it?'

'My Aristotle's definition in his *Physics*,[1] she said, 'is succinct and close to the truth.'

'In what way?' I asked.

'Whenever something is done for some purpose, and for certain reasons something other than what was intended happens, it is called chance. For example, if someone began to dig the ground in order to cultivate a field and found a cache of buried gold. This is believed to have happened fortuitously, but it does not happen as a result of nothing; it has its own causes, the unforeseen and unexpected conjunction of which have clearly effected the chance event. If the cultivator of the field had not been digging, and if the depositor had not buried his money at that point, the gold would not have been found. These, therefore, are the causes of the fortuitous harvest. It is the result of the conjunction of opposite causes, and not of the intention of the doers. Neither the man who buried the gold, nor the man who was tilling the field intended the discovery of the money, but, as I said, it happens as a result of the coincidence that the one began to dig where the other had buried. We may therefore define chance as an unexpected event due to the conjunction of its causes with action which is done for some purpose. The conjunction and coincidence of the causes is effected by that order which proceeds by the inescapable nexus of causation, descending from the fount of Providence and ordering all things in their own time and place.

'Where Parthians turn to shoot the pressing foe
  In flight amid the rough Armenian hills,

1. II, 4-5.

The Tigris and Euphrates from one source
Flow forth and part at once their branching streams.
Should they together come and make one course,
All that their waters bear would there unite;
There ships would meet and torn up trunks of trees,
And mingling streams would weave haphazard paths,
The random chance of which the fall of land
And downward flow of water yet would rule.
Thus chance which seems to flit with reins all loose
Endures the bit and heeds the rule of law.'

II

'I understand, and I agree it is as you say. But is there room in this chain of close-knit causes for any freedom of the will? Or does the chain of Fate bind even the impulses of the human mind?'

freedom

'There is freedom,' she said. 'For it would be impossible for any rational nature to exist without it. Whatever by nature has the use of reason has the power of judgement to decide each matter. It can distinguish by itself between what to avoid and what to desire. But man pursues what he judges to be desirable and avoids that which he thinks undesirable. So that those creatures who have an innate power of reason also have the freedom to will or not to will, though I do not claim that this freedom is equal in all. Celestial and divine beings possess clear sighted judgement, uncorrupted will, and the power to effect their desires. Human souls are of necessity more free when they continue in the contemplation of the mind of God and less free when they descend to bodies, and less still when they are imprisoned in earthly flesh and blood. They reach an extremity of enslavement when they give themselves up to wickedness and lose possession of their proper reason. Once they have turned their eyes away from the light of truth above to things on a lower and dimmer level, they are soon darkened by the mists of ignorance. Destructive passions torment them, and by yielding and giving in to them, they only aid the slavery they have brought upon themselves and become in a manner prisoners of their own freedom. Even so, this is visible to the eye of Providence as it looks out at all things from eternity and arranges predestined rewards according to each man's merit.

'Homer sings with honied tongue
How the brightly shining sun
All things views and all things hears.[2]
And yet with rays too weak to pierce
Far within he cannot see
The bowels of earth or depths of sea.
Not so the Founder of the world
To Whose high gaze is all unfurled,
Matter's dense solidity,
And cloudy night's obscurity.
What is, what was, what is to be,
In one swift glance His mind can see.
All things by Him alone are seen,
And Him the true sun we should deem.'

III

'Look,' I said, 'there is something even more difficult which I find perplexing and confusing.'

'Tell me,' she said, 'though I can guess what is troubling you.'

'Well, the two seem clean contrary and opposite, God's universal foreknowledge and freedom of the will. If God foresees all things and cannot be mistaken in any way, what Providence has foreseen as a future event must happen. So that if from eternity Providence foreknows not only men's actions but also their thoughts and desires, there will be no freedom of will. No action or desire will be able to exist

2. *Iliad*, 3, 277, etc.

other than that which God's infallible Providence has foreseen. For if they can be changed and made different from how
they were foreseen, there will be no sure foreknowledge of the
future, only an uncertain opinion; and this I do not think can
be believed of God.

'I do not agree with the argument by which some people
believe they can cut this Gordian knot. They say that it is not
because Providence has foreseen something as a future event
that it must happen, but the other way round, that because
something is to happen it cannot be concealed from divine
Providence. In this way the necessity is passed to the other
side. It is not necessary, they say, that what is foreseen must
happen, but it is necessary that what is destined to happen
must be foreseen, as though the point at issue was which is the
cause; does foreknowledge of the future cause the necessity of
events, or necessity cause the foreknowledge? But what I am
trying to show is that, whatever the order of the causes, the
coming to pass of things foreknown is necessary even if the
foreknowledge of future events does not seem to impose the
necessity on them.

'If a man is sitting, it is necessary that the opinion which
concludes that he is sitting is true; and on the other hand, if the
opinion about the man is true, because he is sitting, it is
necessary that he is sitting. There is necessity, therefore, in
both statements; in the one that the man is sitting, and in the
other that the opinion is true. But it is not because the opinion
is true, that the man sits; rather, the opinion is true because
it is preceded by the man's act of sitting. So although the
cause of the truth proceeds from the one side, there is, nevertheless, a common necessity in either side. Clearly the same
reasoning applies to Providence and future events. For even
if it is the case that they are foreseen because they are going to happen and not that they happen because they are
foreseen, it is nonetheless necessary that either future events
be foreseen by God or that things foreseen happen as fore-

seen, and this alone is enough to remove freedom of the will.

'But how absurd it is to say that the occurrence of temporal events is the cause of eternal prescience! Yet the opinion that God foresees the future because it is destined to happen is the same as believing that events of a single occurrence are the cause of that supreme Providence.

'Moreover, just as when I know something is, it is necessary that it be, so when I know that something is to be, it is necessary that it shall be. It comes about, therefore, that the occurrence of the event foreknown cannot be avoided.

'Finally, if anyone thinks something is different from what it is, not only is it not knowledge, but it is a false opinion very far from the truth of knowledge. So, if something is destined to happen in such a way that its occurrence is not certain and necessary, who could foreknow that it is to happen? For just as knowledge is unalloyed by falseness, so that which is comprehended by knowledge cannot be other than as it is comprehended. Indeed, the reason why there is no deception in knowledge is because it is necessary for things to be exactly as knowledge understands them to be.

'The question is, therefore, how can God foreknow that these things will happen, if they are uncertain? If He thinks that they will inevitably happen while the possibility of their non-occurrence exists, He is deceived, and this is something wicked both to think and to say. But if His knowledge that they will happen as they do is of such a kind that He knows they may as equally not happen as happen, what sort of knowledge is this, which comprehends nothing sure or stable? How does it differ from that ridiculous prophecy of Tiresias in Horace's *Satires*[3]

Whatever I say either will be or won't?

3. II, 5, 59.

And how is divine Providence superior to opinion if like men it considers those things uncertain whose occurrence is uncertain? If there can be no uncertainty at that most sure fount of all things, the coming to pass of those things which God firmly foreknows as future events is certain. Therefore, human thoughts and actions have no freedom, because the divine mind in foreseeing all things without being led astray by falseness binds human thoughts and actions to a single manner of occurrence.

'Once this has been admitted, the extent of the disruption of human affairs is obvious. In vain is reward offered to the good and punishment to the bad, because they have not been deserved by any free and willed movement of the mind. That which is now judged most equitable, the punishment of the wicked and the reward of the good, will be seen to be the most unjust of all; for men are driven to good or evil not by their own will but by the fixed necessity of what is to be. Neither vice nor virtue will have had any existence; but all merit will have been mixed up and undifferentiated. Nothing more wicked can be conceived than this, for as the whole order of things is derived from Providence and there is no room for human thoughts, it follows that our wickedness, too, is derived from the Author of all good.

'It is pointless, therefore, to hope for anything or pray to escape anything. What can a man hope for, or pray to escape, when an inflexible bond binds all that can be wished for?

'And so the one and only means of communication between man and God is removed, that is hope and prayer – if indeed we do obtain for the price of due humility the inestimable return of divine grace. And this is the only way by which it seems men can talk with God and join themselves to that inaccessible light before they obtain it, by means of supplication. And if admitting the necessity of future events means believing that hope and prayer have no power, what way will

there be left by which we can be joined and united to that
supreme Lord of the world? Cut off and separated from its
source, the human race, as you were singing just now, will be
destined to grow weak and exhausted.

'What warring cause does thus disjoin
The bonds of things? What God has set
Such enmity between two truths,
That things established separately
Refuse a common yoke to bear?
Or is there no discord of truths
Which ever sure in union join?
Is mind, oppressed by members blind,
In lesser brightness powerless
To see the slender links of things?
Why burns it then with love so great
To learn the secret signs of truth?
Perhaps it knows already what it seeks
To learn? But who still seeks to learn things that
He knows? And if the mind knows not, what does
It then in blindness seek? For who could search
In ignorance for anything, or who
Could look for that which was unknown to him,
And where could he discover it? When found
Could ignorance discern the hidden form?
When once the mind beheld the mind of God
Did it both sum and separate truths perceive?
Now hidden in the body's density
It does not lose all memory of itself.
The many separate truths are lost, yet still
It holds the sum. Therefore who seeks the truth
In neither state will be: he does not know,
And yet he is not wholly ignorant.
So he reflects upon the sum retained
And kept in mind, and thinks of what on high
He saw, that he may add the parts forgot
　　　　To that which he retains.'

IV

Then Philosophy spoke. 'This is an old complaint about Providence. Cicero attacked it vigorously in his treatise *On Divination*,[4] and you yourself have investigated it at great length. But up to now none of you has explained it with sufficient care and rigour. The reason for this blindness is that the operation of human reasoning cannot approach the immediacy of divine foreknowledge. If this immediacy could be understood by some means, all uncertainty would be removed. Later on I will try to explain it and make it clear, once I have first dealt with the matters that are disturbing you.

'Take the case of those who believe that foreknowledge does not impose necessity upon the future, and that freedom of the will is not infringed by foreknowledge. I would like to know why you consider their reasoning ineffective. For the only source of your proof of the predestination of the future is your belief that what is foreknown cannot but happen. Therefore, if – as you were only just now saying – if fore-knowledge does not impose any predestination on the future, why is it that acts of the will are forced to be predestined?

'But for the sake of argument, so that you may see what follows, let us say that there is no foreknowledge. In this case, actions of the will are not forced to be predestined, are they?'

'No.'

'Again, let us say that there is foreknowledge, but that it does not impose any predestination on things; the same freedom of the will remains, I think, absolute and unin-fringed.

'But, you will say, even if it is not the same as predestination of the future, foreknowledge is a sign that the future will inevitably happen. In this case, even if there were no fore-knowledge, everyone would agree that the occurrence of the

4. *De Div.*, II, 8 ff.

future is predestined, since signs indicate what they represent, but don't cause it.

'So the first thing to do is to show that nothing happens other than of necessity, so that foreknowledge may be seen as a sign of this necessity; otherwise, if there is no necessity, that foreknowledge, too, cannot be a sign of something that does not exist. But we all agree that we cannot deduce a proof firmly founded upon reason from signs or arguments imported from without: it must come from arguments that fit together and lead from one to the next.

'It cannot be that what is foreseen as a future event does not come to pass. It would be as if we believed that what Providence foreknows as future events are not going to happen, instead of believing that although they happen, they were not predestined in their own nature. You will easily be able to see it in this way; we see many things before our eyes as they happen, like the actions we see charioteers performing in order to control and drive their chariots, and other things of this sort. But no necessity forces any of them to happen in this way, does it?'

'No, for if they all happened of necessity the exercise of skill would be futile.'

'Therefore, all those things which happen without happening of necessity are, before they happen, future events about to happen, but not about to happen of necessity. For just as the knowledge of present things imposes no necessity on what is happening, so foreknowledge imposes no necessity on what is going to happen.

'But this, you will say, is the very point in question – whether there can be any foreknowledge of things whose occurrence is not inevitable. There seems to be a contradiction here, and you think that the necessity of events is consequent upon their being foreseen, while if there is no necessity, they cannot be foreknown, because you believe that nothing can be comprehended by knowledge unless it is certain. If events of uncertain occurrence are foreseen as if they were certain, it is only clouded opinion, not the truth of knowledge; for you believe that to have opinions about something which differ from the actual facts is not the same as the fulness of knowledge.

'The cause of this mistake is that people think that the totality of their knowledge depends on the nature and capacity to be known of the objects of knowledge. But this is all wrong. Everything that is known is comprehended not according to its own nature, but according to the ability to know of those who do the knowing. Let us make it clear with a brief example; the same roundness of shape is recognized in one way by the sight and in another way by the touch. The sight remains at a distance and sees the whole simultaneously by means of rays of light passing from the eye, while the touch coming close to and grasping the sphere perceives its roundness part by part. Similarly man himself is beheld in different ways by sense-perception, imagination, reason and intelligence.[5] The senses examine his shape as constituted in matter, while imagination considers his shape alone without

5. 'Intelligence' (Latin *intelligentia*) in this passage bears a technical sense related to the two faculties which the rational soul was supposed to exercise, 'intellect' (*intellectus*) and 'reason' (*ratio*). 'Intellect' here means 'understanding' and is that imperfect faculty in corporeal man which corresponds to the perfect 'intelligence' of incorporeal angels: its relation to 'reason' is ex plained by St Thomas Aquinas (I[a], lxxxix, art. 8) as follows (quoted from *The Discarded Image*, p. 157): 'intellect (*intelligere*) is the simple (i.e. indivisible, uncompounded) grasp of an intelligible truth, whereas reasoning (*ratiocinari*) is the progression towards an intelligible truth by going from one understood (*intellecto*) point to another. The difference between them is thus like the difference between rest and motion or between possession and acquisition.' C. S. Lewis continues (loc. cit.): 'We are enjoying *intellectus* when we "just see" a self-evident truth; we are exercising *ratio* when we proceed step by step to prove a truth which is not self-evident. A cognitive life in which all truth can be simply "seen" would be the life of an *intelligentia*, an angel. A life of unmitigated *ratio* where nothing was simply "seen" and all had to be proved, would presumably be impossible; for nothing can be proved if nothing is self-evident. Man's mental life is spent in laboriously connecting those frequent, but momentary, flashes of *intelligentia* which constitute *intellectus*.'

matter. Reason transcends imagination, too, and with a universal consideration reflects upon the species inherent in individual instances. But there exists the more exalted eye of intelligence which passes beyond the sphere of the universe to behold the simple form itself with the pure vision of the mind.[6]

'The point of greatest importance here is this: the superior manner of knowledge includes the inferior, but it is quite impossible for the inferior to rise to the superior. The senses cannot perceive anything beyond matter; imagination does

6. The source of this argument that knowledge depends on the capacity of the knower to know, and not the capacity of the object to be known, is in the writings of Iamblichus, Ammonius and Proclus. Two terms in the passage need a short comment: *universal* and *form*. Of the former Aristotle says, 'By the term *universal* I mean that which is of such a nature as to be predicated of many subjects' (*De Interpretatione*, 17a), e.g. the concept 'horse' as opposed to many individual horses. But for Aristotle the *universal* was not just a subjective concept; it was something real both in the mind and in things. 'Strictly speaking, there is no objective Universal for Aristotle, but there is an objective foundation in things for the subjective universal in the mind. The universal "horse" is a subjective concept, but it has an objective foundation in the substantial forms that inform particular horses.' (F. Copleston, *A History of philosophy*, I, ch. 29.) Similarly for Plato, the *universal*, to which he gave the name *idea* or *form*, was something real, but unlike Aristotle Plato accorded the *form* a separate substance in a non-sensible world of 'real reality' different from the unreal everyday world of sense perception. The use of the word *form* in this passage seems to be closer to St Augustine, who follows the Middle Academy and Plotinus, than to Plato: cf. the words of Boyer, *L'Idée de la Verité*, quoted by M. C. D'Arcy, S. J., in his essay on St Augustine's philosophy in *A Monument to St Augustine*, London, 1930 (reprinted as *St Augustine* by Meridian Books, 1957): 'Our intellect is, in fact, nothing else than the divine Light tempered to the infirmity of our nature. The truths we see are partial, limited, made clumsy by the multiplicity of the terms. Nevertheless, they are the expression, suited to our nature, of the total and simple truth, which is God. No one of our ideas, whatever we do, reveals to us the pure Idea which is in God, but each of our ideas, in its positive content, expresses something which belongs to God, although under a form which the idea does not reveal.' The 'simple form' – or pure idea – which is the subject of the knowledge of intelligence is like the Augustinian forms in the mind of God, that is, in Christ, the Divine Wisdom. 'There are certain ideas,' he writes in *De diversis questionibus*, 83, q.46, 'forms, or reasons, of things which are immutable and constant, which are immaterial and contained in the divine intellect . . .'

not consider universal species; and reason does not comprehend simple form; but intelligence as though looking down from above, first perceives form and then distinguishes all things that are under it, but in such a way that it comprehends the form itself which could not be known to any other. It knows reason's knowledge of universals, imagination's knowledge of shape, and the senses' knowledge of matter without using reason, imagination, or the senses, but by the single glance of the mind according to the form, so to speak, as it looks out at all things. Reason, too, when it looks at some universal, without using imagination or the senses, comprehends the imaginable and sensible objects of both. Reason it is that so defines the universal concept; man is a biped rational animal. Since this is a universal concept, everyone knows it is a concept which can be both imagined and perceived by the senses, while reason considers it not through imagination or the senses, but through rational comprehension. Imagination, too, may have taken its original power to see and form figures from the senses, yet in the absence of the senses it can still survey all sensible objects not through sensory but through imaginative perception.

'So you see, in their manner of knowing they all use their own capacity to know rather than the capacity to be known of the objects of their knowledge. And this is quite proper. For since every judgement is an action of the one who judges, it is necessary that each should perform its work by its own power and not another's.

'The Stoics of the Painted Porch[7]
Once taught obscure philosophers
To think of things the senses learn

7. The Stoics take their name from the Painted Stoa or Colonnade at Athens where Zeno of Citium (335–263 B.C.), the founder of Stoicism, carried on his teaching. Stoicism was a materialist philosophy; only bodies had a real substantial existence, and the Stoic theory of knowledge was, therefore, an account of how the soul, itself a body, was affected by other bodies – the things

As images impressed upon
The mind from bodies round about;
Just as with swiftly moving pen
It was the custom once to print
Upon the spreading sea of wax
Untouched as yet by mark or scratch
Written letters deep impressed.
But if the active mind of its
Own power can nothing learn or find,
But lies all passive to receive
The imprint of bodies from without;
If like a mirror it reflects
The empty images of things;
Whence comes to minds this concept strong
Which thus discerns and sees all things?
What power can individuals see,
First analyse that which it sees,
Then synthesize analysis
And by alternate paths progress?
Now lift its head to highest things,
Now down to lowest fall again;
Now turning back unto itself
False things with true things overthrow?
This is a cause more powerful,
More forceful and effectual
Than that which passively awaits
The print of matter from without:
And yet passivity in things
That live precedes the calling forth
And stirring of the power of mind;

that are known. Cleanthes (331–232), who succeeded Zeno, actually used the metaphor of a seal impressed on wax to describe the impression an object makes on the soul in sense-perception. There was no place in this materialist system for objectively existing universals like Plato's *forms*. The active power of mind which Boethius opposes to this theory of passive receptivity seems to owe something to Aristotle's problematic Active Reason. (See A. H. Armstrong, *An Introduction to Ancient Philosophy*, University Paperbacks, 1965, pp. 96–7.)

As when light strikes upon the eye
Or voices clatter in the ear:
The active power of mind then roused
Calls forth the species from within
To motions of a similar kind;
And fitting them to marks impressed
From outside, mingles images
Received with forms it hides within.'

V

'But if in the perception of corporeal phenomena external
stimuli strike and impinge on the instruments of the senses,
and corporeal passivity precedes mental activity – a passivity
which stimulates mental activity and calls up the dormant
forms in the mind – if, I say, in perceiving corporeal phenomena the mind is not passively affected, but judges of its own
power the experience subjected to the body, consider the case
of beings which in their mode of perception are free from all
corporeal influence. They can rouse their mind to activity
without having to react to external stimuli in order to perceive
things. By this argument, therefore, a multiplicity of kinds of
knowledge has been given to different substances. Mere
sensation without any other kind of knowing has been given
to animals that have no power of movement, like mussels and
other shellfish which grow on rocks. Imagination has been
given to animals which do have the power of movement and
which appear to have some will to choose or avoid things.
Reason belongs only to the human race, just as intelligence
belongs only to divinity. The result is that that kind of
knowing transcends the others which of its own nature
knows not only its own objects, but also the objects of the
other kinds of knowing.
'Suppose, then, the senses and the imagination opposed
reason and said that the universal that reason thought she
could see was nothing at all, on the grounds that what is

sensible or imaginable cannot be universal; and that either therefore the judgement of reason was true, and that there was nothing sensible, or, since reason knew that many things were objects of the senses and the imagination, reason's manner of knowing was worthless, because it thought of that which was sensible and individual as a kind of universal. If, moreover, reason should reply in answer that in considering what was universal she kept in sight that which was comprehended by the senses and that which was comprehended by the imagination, but that the senses and the imagination could not rise to the recognition of universality because their manner of knowing could not go beyond corporeal shapes: and if she added that in the matter of the way things are known, credence should be given to the more sure and perfect discernment; in an argument like this, we, being persons who have the ability to reason as well as to imagine and perceive by the senses, would surely approve of the case of reason.

'In the same way, human reason refuses to believe that divine intelligence can see the future in any other way except that in which human reason has knowledge. This is how the argument runs: if anything does not seem to have any certain and predestined occurrence, it cannot be foreknown as a future event. Of such, therefore, there is no foreknowledge: and if we believe that even in this case there is foreknowledge, there will be nothing which does not happen of necessity. If, therefore, as beings who have a share of reason, we can judge of the mind of God, we should consider it most fitting for human reason to bow before divine wisdom, just as we judged it right for the senses and the imagination to yield to reason.

'Let us, then, if we can, raise ourselves up to the heights of that supreme intelligence. There reason will be able to see that which it cannot see by itself – it will be able to see how that which has no certain occurrence may be seen by a certain and fixed foreknowledge, a knowledge that is not opinion, but the boundless immediacy of the highest form of knowing.

'How many different shapes of life across the world!
Sometimes in elongated form it sweeps the dirt
And draws unbroken furrows borne on powerful ribs;
Sometimes on wandering wings it lightly beats the winds
And swims in liquid flight through airy tracts of space;
Some forms press footprints on the earth and step by step
Transport them over fields or under forest sides.
In different shapes you see them all, yet each one's look
Is downward to the ground directed, dulling sense;
Alone the race of men can lift its head on high,
Can stand with body upright and disdain the ground.
This picture warns – except to doltish earthbound men –
"You who raise your eyes to heaven with thrusting face,
Raise up as well your thoughts, lest weighted down to earth
Your mind sinks lower as your body rises high." '[8]

VI

'Since, therefore, as we have just shown, every object of knowledge is known not as a result of its own nature, but of the nature of those who comprehend it, let us now examine, as far as we may, the nature of the divine substance, so that we may also learn what is its mode of knowledge.

'It is the common judgement, then, of all creatures that live by reason that God is eternal. So let us consider the nature of eternity, for this will make clear to us both the nature of God and his manner of knowing.[9] Eternity, then, is the complete, simultaneous and perfect possession of everlasting life; this will be clear from a comparison with creatures that exist in

8. With deliberate artistry Boethius recalls – and contrasts – the picture of the sufferer contemplating with downcast eyes the lowly dust in I, 2.

9. For much of the following section Boethius follows his Neo-platonist sources: but his exultant definition (cf. Helen Waddell, *The Wandering Scholars*, Pelican Books, 1954, p. 27) of eternity is remarkably close to the view of St Augustine. For him the universe was not created in time, but with time. In virtue of His eternity, God transcends time. Created things came into existence only in time. God knew them before their creation and it is in virtue of this eternal act of knowledge that He can foresee and know beforehand even the free acts of men. Cf. Copleston, op. cit., II, ch. 5, sections 4 and 5.

time. Whatever lives in time exists in the present and progresses from the past to the future, and there is nothing set in
time which can embrace simultaneously the whole extent of
its life: it is in the position of not yet possessing tomorrow
when it has already lost yesterday. In this life of today you do
not live more fully than in that fleeting and transitory moment.
Whatever, therefore, suffers the condition of being in time,
even though it never had any beginning, never has any ending
and its life extends into the infinity of time, as Aristotle
thought was the case of the world, it is still not such that it
may properly be considered eternal.

'Its life may be infinitely long, but it does not embrace and
comprehend its whole extent simultaneously. It still lacks the
future, while already having lost the past. So that that which
embraces and possesses simultaneously the whole fullness of
everlasting life, which lacks nothing of the future and has lost
nothing of the past, that is what may properly be said to be
eternal. Of necessity it will always be present to itself, controlling itself, and have present the infinity of fleeting time.

'Those philosophers are wrong, therefore, who when told
that Plato believed the world had had no beginning in time
and would have no end, maintain that the created world is
co-eternal with the Creator. For it is one thing to progress
like the world in Plato's theory through everlasting life, and
another thing to have embraced the whole of everlasting
life in one simultaneous present. This is clearly a property of the mind of God. God ought not to be considered
as older than the created world in extent of time, but rather in
the property of the immediacy of His nature. The infinite
changing of things in time is an attempt to imitate this state
of the presence of unchanging life, but since it cannot portray
or equal that state it falls from sameness into change, from the
immediacy of presence into the infinite extent of past and
future. It cannot possess simultaneously the whole fullness of its
life, but by the very fact that it is impossible for its existence

ever to come to an end, it does seem in some measure to emulate that which it cannot fulfil or express. It does this by attaching itself to some sort of presence in this small and fleeting moment, and since this presence bears a certain resemblance to that abiding present, it confers on whatever possesses it the appearance of being that which it imitates.

'But since it could not remain, it seized upon the infinite journey through time, and in this way it became possible for it to continue by progression forward that life whose fullness it could not embrace by remaining still. And so, if we want to give things their proper names, let us follow Plato and say that God is eternal, the world perpetual.

'Since, therefore, all judgement comprehends those things that are subject to it according to its own nature, and since the state of God is ever that of eternal presence, His knowledge, too, transcends all temporal change and abides in the immediacy of His presence. It embraces all the infinite recesses of past and future and views them in the immediacy of its knowing as though they are happening in the present. If you wish to consider, then, the foreknowledge or prevision by which He discovers all things, it will be more correct to think of it not as a kind of foreknowledge of the future, but as the knowledge of a never ending presence. So that it is better called providence or "looking forth" than prevision or "seeing beforehand". For it is far removed from matters below and looks forth at all things as though from a lofty peak above them.

'Why, then, do you insist that all that is scanned by the sight of God becomes necessary? Men see things but this certainly doesn't make them necessary. And your seeing them doesn't impose any necessity on the things you see present, does it?'

'No.'

'And if human and divine present may be compared, just as you see certain things in this your present time, so God sees all things in His eternal present. So that this divine fore-knowledge does not change the nature and property of things; it simply sees things present to it exactly as they will happen at some time as future events. It makes no confused judgements of things, but with one glance of its mind distinguishes all that is to come to pass whether it is necessitated or not. Similarly you, when you see at the same time a man walking on the earth and the sun rising in the sky, although the two sights coincide yet you distinguish between them and judge the one to be willed and the other necessitated. In the same way the divine gaze looks down on all things without disturbing their nature; to Him they are present things, but under the condition of time they are future things. And so it comes about that when God knows that something is going to occur and knows that no necessity to be is imposed upon it, it is not opinion, but rather knowledge founded upon truth.

'If you say at this point that what God sees as a future event cannot but happen, and what cannot but happen, happens of necessity, and if you bind me to this word necessity, I shall have to admit that it is a matter of the firmest truth, but one which scarcely anyone except a student of divinity has been able to fathom. I shall answer that the same future event is necessary when considered with reference to divine fore-knowledge, and yet seems to be completely free and unrestricted when considered in itself. For there are two kinds of necessity;[10] one simple, as for example the fact that it is necessary that all men are mortal; and one conditional, as for

---

10. For his distinction between simple and conditional or hypothetical necessity, Boethius relies ultimately on Aristotle. The distinction is parallel to that already used by Boethius and likewise derived from Aristotle – along with the example of the buried gold – between absolute and incidental causes in the explanation of chance in Chapter 1 of book V. For a full and illuminating analysis of the way in which Boethius turns at the end of his work from the Platonic to the Aristotelian tradition for his final solution of the problem of necessity and free will, see H. R. Patch, *Necessity in Boethius and the Neoplatonists*, in *Speculum*, X, 1935, pp. 393–404.

example, if you know someone is walking, it is necessary that he is walking. For that which a man knows cannot be other than as it is known; but this conditional necessity does not imply simple necessity, because it does not exist in virtue of its own nature, but in virtue of a condition which is added. No necessity forces the man to walk who is making his way of his own free will, although it is necessary that he walks when he takes a step.

'In the same way, if Providence sees something as present, it is necessary for it to happen, even though it has no necessity in its own nature. God sees those future events which happen of free will as present events; so that these things when considered with reference to God's sight of them do happen necessarily as a result of the condition of divine knowledge; but when considered in themselves they do not lose the absolute freedom of their nature. All things, therefore, whose future occurrence is known to God do without doubt happen, but some of them are the result of free will. In spite of the fact that they do happen, their existence does not deprive them of their true nature, in virtue of which the possibility of their non-occurrence existed before they happened.

'What does it matter, then, if they are not necessary, when because of the condition of divine foreknowledge it will turn out exactly as if they were necessary? The answer is this. It is impossible for the two events I mentioned just now – the rising of the sun and the man walking – not to be happening when they do happen; and yet it was necessary for one of them to happen before it did happen, but not so for the other. And so, those things which are present to God will without doubt happen; but some of them result from the necessity of things, and some of them from the power of those who do them. We are not wrong, therefore, to say that if these things are considered with reference to divine foreknowledge, they are necessary, but if they are considered by themselves, they are free of the bonds of necessity; just as everything that the senses perceive is universal if considered with reference to the reason, but individual if considered in itself.

'But, you will reply, if it lies in my power to change a proposed course of action, I will be able to evade Providence, for I will perhaps have altered things which Providence foreknows. My answer will be that you can alter your plan, but that since this is possible, and since whether you do so or in what way you change it is visible to Providence the ever present and true, you cannot escape divine foreknowledge, just as you cannot escape the sight of an eye that is present to watch, though of your own free will you may turn to a variety of actions.

'Well, you will ask, isn't divine knowledge changed as a result of my rearrangement, so that as I change my wishes it, too, seems to change its knowledge? The answer is no. Each future thing is anticipated by the gaze of God which bends it back and recalls it to the presence of its own manner of knowledge; it does not change, as you think, with alternate knowledge of now this and now that, but with one glance anticipates and embraces your changes in its constancy. God receives this present mode of knowledge and vision of all things not from the issue of future things but from His own immediacy. So that the difficulty you put forward a short time ago,[11] that it was unfitting if our future is said to provide a cause of God's knowledge, is solved. The power of this knowledge which embraces all things in present understanding has itself set a limit upon things and owes nothing to events which come after it. And since this is so, man's freedom of will remains inviolate and the law does not impose reward and punishment unfairly, because the will is free from all necessity. God has foreknowledge and rests a spectator from on high of all things; and as the ever present eternity of His vision dispenses reward to the good and punishment to the bad, it adapts itself to the future quality of our actions. Hope is not

II. V, chapter 3, p. 152.

placed in God in vain and prayers are not made in vain, for if they are the right kind they cannot but be efficacious. Avoid vice, therefore, and cultivate virtue; lift up your mind to the right kind of hope, and put forth humble prayers on high. A great necessity is laid upon you, if you will be honest with yourself, a great necessity to be good, since you live in the sight of a judge who sees all things.'

BIBLIOGRAPHY

This list contains references to the books I have consulted: a fuller bibliography may be found in Bieler's edition of the *Consolation*.

ARMSTRONG, A. H., *An Introduction to Ancient Philosophy*, 3rd ed., London, 1957 (reprinted in University Paperbacks, 1965).

BARRETT, H. M., *Boethius: some aspects of his times and work*, Cambridge, 1940.

Boethii Philosophiae Consolationis libri quinque, ed. Guilelmus Weinberger, *Corpus Scriptorum Ecclesiasticorum Latinorum*, LXVII, Vindobonae/Lipsiae, 1934.

Boethii Philosophiae Consolatio, ed. Ludovicus Bieler, *Corpus Christianorum* Series Latina XCIV, Turnholti, 1957.

BOETHIUS, *Theological Tractates and Consolation of Philosophy*, ed. H. F. Stewart and E. K. Rand, Loeb Classical Library, 1918.

BOETHIUS, *Consolation of Philosophy*, translated by W. V. Cooper, Temple Classics, London, 1902.

BULLOUGH, DONALD, *Germanic Italy* in *The Dark Ages*, ed. D. T. Rice, London, 1965.

CAMPENHAUSEN, HANS VON, *The Fathers of the Latin Church*, translated by Manfred Hoffman, London, 1964.

CAPPUYNS, M., *Boèce* in *Dictionnaire d'Histoire et de Géographie Ecclésiastique*, IX, 1937, col. 348–80.

CASSIODORUS, *The Letters*, translated by T. Hodgkin, London, 1886.

Catulli Carmina, ed. R. A. B. Mynors, Oxford, 1958.

CATULLUS, *The Poems*, translated by Peter Whigham, Penguin Books, 1966.

CHAUCER, GEOFFREY, *The Works*, ed. F. N. Robinson, 2nd ed., London, 1957.

CHAUCER, *Translation of Boethius de Consolatione Philosophiae*, ed. R. Morris, Early English Text Society, Extra Series V, 1868.

CICERO, *Somnium Scipionis*, ed. C. Meissner and G. Landgraf, Leipzig, 1915, repr. Amsterdam, 1964.

COOK, A. B., *Zeus, Jupiter and the Oak*, Classical Review, XVII, 1903.

COOPER, L., *A Concordance to Boethius*, Cambridge, Mass., 1928.

COPLESTON, F., *A History of Philosophy*, Image Books edition, 1962.

CROMBIE, A. C., *Augustine to Galileo*, Mercury Books ed., London, 1961.

CURTIUS, E. R., *European Literature and the Latin Middle Ages*, translated by W. R. Trask, Bollingen Series, XXXVI, 1953.

DANTE, *The Divine Comedy: Paradise*, translated by Dorothy L. Sayers and Barbara Reynolds, Penguin Books, 1962.

D'ARCY, M. C., *The Philosophy of St Augustine* in *St Augustine, His Age, Life and Thought*, Meridian Books, 1957 (originally published as *A Monument to St Augustine*, London, 1930).

DIOGENES LAERTIUS, *Lives of eminent philosophers*, translated by R. D. Hicks, Loeb Classical Library, 2 vols., 1925.

FAVEZ, C., *La Consolation Latine Chrétienne*, Paris, 1937.

FEHLAUER, F., *Die englischen Übersetzungen von Boethius' De Consolatione Philosophiae*, Normania 2, Berlin, 1909.

FIELD, G. C., *The Philosophy of Plato*, London, 1949.

FORDYCE, C. J., *Catullus, A Commentary*, Oxford, 1961.

FOX, A., *Plato for Pleasure*, London, 1945.

GIBBON, *The Decline and Fall of the Roman Empire*, ed. J. B. Bury, London, 1898.

GRAVES, R., *The Greek Myths*, 2 vols., Penguin Books, 1955.

HOMER, *The Iliad*, translated by E. V. Rieu, Penguin Classics, 1950.

HODGKIN, T., *Italy and Her Invaders*, vol. III *The Ostrogothic Invasion*, Oxford, 1885.

JUVENAL and PERSIUS, ed. G. G. Ramsay, Loeb Classical Library, 1918.

JUVENAL, *The Sixteen Satires*, translated by Peter Green, Penguin Classics, 1967.

KER, W. P., *The Dark Ages*, Edinburgh/London, 1923.

KLINGNER, F., *De Boethii Consolatione Philosophiae*, 2. Unveranderte Auflage, Zürich/Dublin, 1966.

KNOWLES, D., *The Evolution of Mediaeval Thought*, London, 1962.

Lactanti De Ira Dei liber ed. in *Opera Omnia* II i by S. Brandt and G. Laubman, *Corpus Scriptorum Ecclesiasticorum Latinorum*, Vindobonae, 1893.

LEFF, GORDON, *Medieval Thought: St Augustine to Ockham*, London, 1958.

LEWIS, C. S., *The Allegory of Love*, Oxford, 1936.

LEWIS, C. S., *The Discarded Image*, Cambridge, 1964.

LUCAN, *Pharsalia*, translated by Robert Graves, Penguin Classics, 1956.

MÂLE, ÉMILE, *The Gothic Image*, translated by Dora Hussey, Fontana Library, 1961.

MIGNE, *Patrologia Latina*.

PATCH, H. R., *The Goddess Fortuna in Medieval Literature*, Cambridge, Mass., 1927.

PATCH, H. R., *Fate in Boethius and the Neoplatonists*, Speculum IV, 1929, pp. 62–72.

PATCH, H. R., *Consolatio Philosophiae IV m. vi*, 23–24, Speculum VIII, 1933, pp. 41–51.

PATCH, H. R., *Necessity in Boethius and the Neoplatonists*, Speculum X, 1935, pp 393–404.

PATCH, H. R., *The Tradition of Boethius; A Study of his Importance in Medieval Culture*, New York/Oxford, 1935.

PICKERING, F. P., *Notes on Fate and Fortune in Mediaeval German Studies Presented to Frederick Norman*, London, 1965, pp. 1–15.

PLATO, *The Symposium*, translated by W. Hamilton, Penguin Classics, 1951.

PLATO, *The Last Days of Socrates*, translated by Hugh Tredennick, Penguin Classics, 1954.

PLATO, *The Protagoras and Meno*, translated by W. K. C. Guthrie, Penguin Classics, 1956.

PLATO, *The Timaeus*, translated by H. D. P. Lee, Penguin Classics, 1965.

PLUTARCH, *Moralia*, translated by P. H. de Lacy and B. Einarson, Loeb Classical Library, 1959.

RABY, F. J. E., *A History of Christian Latin Poetry*, 2nd ed., Oxford, 1953.

RAND, E. K., *Founders of the Middle Ages*, Harvard, 1929.

ROBINSON, D. M., *The Wheel of Fortune*, Classical Philology, XLI, 1946.

ROSS, W. D., *Aristotle*, London, 1923.

Scriptores Historiae Augustae translated by David Magie, Loeb Classical Library, 1924.

SICILIANO, ITALO, *François Villon et les thèmes poétiques du moyen âge*, Paris, 1934.

SMITH, K. F., *The Elegies of Albus Tibullus*, Darmstadt, 1964.

STEWART, H. F., *Boethius – An Essay*, Edinburgh/London, 1891.

SUETONIUS, *The Twelve Caesars*, translated by Robert Graves, Penguin Classics, 1957.

TACITUS, *On Imperial Rome*, translated by Michael Grant, Penguin Classics, 1956.

TAYLOR, A. E., *Plato; the Man and His Work*, London, 1926.

VANN, GERALD, *A Note on Boethius* in *Moral Dilemmas*, London, 1965.

WADDELL, HELEN, *The Wandering Scholars*, Penguin Books, 1954.

The Oxford Classical Dictionary, ed. M. Cary and others, Oxford, 1949.

The Oxford Dictionary of the Christian Church, ed. F. L. Cross, London, 1957.

Pauly-Wissowa, *Real-Encyclopädie*.

GLOSSARY

of Proper Names mentioned in the
Introduction, Text and Notes

Acacius, Patriarch of Constantinople, A.D. 471–489. He was probably
the author of the Emperor Zeno's *Henoticon*, a theological formula
intended to bring about union between the orthodox and the
Monophysites. The formula was not accepted in Rome and led
to a temporary schism (482–519) between East and West known as
the Acacian schism.

Achelous, name of a river in Greece and of its god; see note p. 146.

Aemilius Paulus, see *Paulus*.

Agamemnon, mythological son of Atreus and in Homer commander-
in-chief of the Greek expedition to Troy. See note p. 145.

Agrippina, known as Agrippina Minor; mother of the Emperor Nero
whom she persuaded her third husband, the Emperor Claudius, to
adopt. She was murdered on Nero's instructions in A.D. 59. See
Tacitus, *Annals*, 12–14.

Albinus, a Roman of consular rank accused by Cyprian of treason.
His defence by Boethius led Cyprian to extend the charge to him
as well.

Alcibiades, Athenian general (c. 450–404 B.C.). He was a pupil and
friend of Socrates, and famous for his brilliant but disastrous career
and for his physical beauty. See note p. 92.

Ammonius, mystical philosopher (third century A.D.). Through his
influence on his pupil Plotinus he is regarded as one of the founders
of Neoplatonism.

Anastasius, Emperor of the East, A.D. 491–518.

Anaxagoras of Clazomenae, one of the earliest philosophers to settle in
Athens (c. 500–c. 428 B.C.). He was brought to trial on charges of
impiety and treachery but escaped with the aid of friends.

Anaxarchus of Abdera, sceptic philosopher (fourth century B.C.). He was
cruelly put to death by Nicocreon of Cyprus. See note p. 70.

Antaeus, a mythological giant who forced everyone he met to wrestle with him, and then killed them. Eventually he was himself defeated and killed by Hercules. See note p. 146.

Arcadian God, see *Hermes*.

Arianism, a Christian heresy which taught the divinity of the Father but not of the Son. The Goths were Arians.

Aristotle, Greek philosopher (384–322 B.C.) and founder of the peripatetic school. See Introduction, pp. 12–13.

Atreus, mythological father of Agamemnon.

Augustine, saint, philosopher, theologian, bishop of Hippo (A.D. 354–430). He was born and educated in North Africa, came to Rome in 383 and became professor of rhetoric at Milan in 384 where he came under the influence of St Ambrose and was baptized in 386. He was greatly influenced by Neoplatonism and through his writings (which include *The Confessions* and *The City of God*) exercised the greatest influence on Christian thought of any of the Latin fathers.

Basilius, a Roman of doubtful reputation who was one of Boethius' accusers. He may be the same as the Basilius who was accused along with Praetextatus of magical practices (Cassiodorus, *Variae* 4, 22 and 23), but the identification is uncertain.

Boethius, Anicius Manlius Severinus, Roman senator, philosopher and minister of Theodoric (*c*.480–524 or 5 A.D.). See Introduction, pp. 9 ff.

Britannicus, Tiberius Claudius Caesar, son of the Emperor Claudius (A.D. 41–55). His stepmother Agrippina contrived that her own son Nero should succeed Claudius and according to general belief Britannicus was poisoned on Nero's orders. See note p. 72.

Brutus, Marcus Junius, the tyrannicide who took part in the murder of Julius Caesar 44 B.C. Like Cato and Fabricius he was famous for his moral uprightness and virtue.

Burgundians, a once powerful East Germanic people which had settled in the Rhône valley.

Busiris, a mythological king of Egypt reputed to sacrifice to Zeus all foreigners who entered Egypt. He was defeated and killed by Hercules.

Cacus, in mythology a savage fire-breathing monster who lived on the site of Rome and ravaged the neighbourhood. He was overcome and killed by Hercules when he stole the cattle of Geryon from him. See note p. 146, and Virgil *Aen.* 8, 190 ff.

Caesar, Gaius Julius, Roman general and dictator murdered by Brutus and others (102–44 B.C.).

Caligula, nickname by which the Emperor Gaius (A.D. 12–41) was known. He was the most autocratic of the early emperors.

Campania, a province of Italy extending from Rome to Salerno; roughly the modern Campagna.

Canius, probably the Stoic philosopher Julius Canus condemned to death by Caligula and cited by Seneca as an example of philosophic tranquillity (*De Tranquilitate* 14, 4 ff).

Caracalla, usual name of the Emperor Marcus Aurelius Antoninus (A.D. 188–217). He had his brother and many distinguished men of state put to death.

Carthaginians, inhabitants of the North African city of Carthage, one of the great rivals of Rome in the Republican period. The Punic wars of the third and second centuries B.C. saw Rome gradually supersede Carthage as the chief Mediterranean power.

Cassiodorus, Flavius Magnus Aurelius, Roman statesman, historian, encyclopedist, theologian and monk (*c.* A.D. 480–*c.*575). He served Theodoric and his successors in the highest offices of state in a position equivalent to that of Prime Minister, and his collected letters (the *Variae*) are a chief source for the history of the time. When Ravenna was captured for Justinian by Belisarius in 540 and Gothic rule in Italy came to an end, Cassiodorus retired to a monastery he founded near his native Squillace in Calabria, where he was able to realize his educational interests. The programme of manuscript copying he instituted preserved for the world the pagan classical authors whose work was in danger of perishing. He was the most important sixth-century writer after Boethius. See Hodgkin's edition of the *Letters* and E. K. Rand, *Founders of the Middle Ages*, pp. 240 ff.

Cato Uticensis, Marcus Porcius, Roman aristocrat, politician and Stoic, famous for his stern traditional morality (95–46 B.C.). His character in Lucan is a personification of virtue.

Catullus, Gaius Valerius, Roman poet, writer mainly of short lyric, erotic, abusive and epigrammatic poems (*c.*84–*c.*54 B.C.). See note p. 85.

Caucasus, a chain of mountains stretching from the Black Sea to the Caspian, regarded as the extremity of the world.

Centaurs, a race of mythical monsters half man and half horse. See note p. 146.

Cerberus, mythological monstrous dog guarding the entrance to Hades. The usual representation showed him with three heads and a mane or tail of snakes.

Cicero, Marcus Tullius, Roman orator, philosopher and writer of letters (106–43 B.C.). Boethius is greatly indebted to Cicero, quoting from philosophical works of his like the *Dream of Scipio* and the lost *Hortensius*: it was this latter work which first fired St Augustine's passionate interest in philosophy. Boethius was following Cicero's example in planning the translation of Greek philosophical works into Latin.

Circe, a mythological goddess encountered by Odysseus on his return journey from Troy. See note p. 126, and Homer *Odyssey*, 10, 210 ff.

Claudian (Claudius Claudianus), one of the last great Latin classic poets (d. *c.* A.D. 408).

Clovis (Chlodovechus), king of the Franks (*c.* A.D. 466–511). He was nominated consul by the Eastern Emperor Anastasius in 508.

Conigast or *Cunigast*, a Gothic minister of Theodoric and later of his grandson Athalaric, accused by Boethius of oppressing the poor.

Croesus, wealthy and powerful king of Lydia (reigned *c.*560–546 B.C.). His meeting with the Greek sage Solon was famous for the reply given by the latter to the question who was the happiest man he had ever seen. Solon said that no man should be considered happy until he had ended his life in a happy way. Croesus was eventually defeated and captured by Cyrus, and when about to be burnt alive called three times on the name of Solon. Cyrus inquired the identity of this Solon and on hearing the story, had Croesus released.

Cyclops, one of a mythological race of one-eyed giants, the most famous of whom was Polyphemus. See note p. 145.

Cyprian, a Roman of noble birth, one of those who allied themselves to the Goths, accuser of Albinus and Boethius. At the time he was *referendarius* in the king's court of appeal and a loyal and favourite servant of Theodoric. Boethius calls him an informer moved by hatred, but according to Cassiodorus Cyprian's impartiality was admired by litigants (*Variae* 5, 40) and he is praised in glowing terms. It was probably on a mission to the Byzantine court that he first unearthed the intrigues of the pro-Eastern circle in Rome. In 524 he was appointed Count of the Sacred Largesses and eventually promoted to the dignity of *patricius*.

Cyrus, founder of the Achaemenid Persian Empire and conqueror of Croesus of Lydia (reigned 559–529 B.C.). See p. 57 and Herodotus 1, 71 ff.

Damocles, a courtier of Dionysius I of Syracuse. On one occasion when he spoke with exaggeration of the wealth and happiness of Dionysius, as a symbol of the uncertainty of his position Dionysius gave a sumptuous feast for him at which he had to sit with a sword suspended over his head by a single hair. See Cicero, *Tusc.*, 5, 61.

Decoratus, a young noble Roman advocate, appointed *quaestor* probably along with Boethius some time before 509, the year of his death. Boethius speaks of him with contempt, but both Ennodius and Cassiodorus praise him for his excellent qualities.

Diomedes, mythological king of the Bistones; the eighth labour of Hercules was to capture his man-eating horses. See note p. 146.

Dionysius I, tyrant of Syracuse (c.430–367 B.C.).

Empedocles, Sicilian philosopher of considerable importance in the development of Greek philosophy (c.493–433 B.C.). According to him cosmic history is a cyclic process of the combination and dissolution under the alternate influence of Love and Strife of the four eternally unchanging elements earth, air, fire and water.

Ennodius, Magnus Felix, saint, Christian rhetorician, bishop of Pavia, writer of letters, speeches and poems (A.D. 473/4–521). He taught rhetoric at Milan until his ordination as bishop in c.514. The chief characteristic of his writings is the turgidity of their style.

Epicureanism see *Epicurus*.

Epicurus, famous Athenian philosopher (342/1–271/70 B.C.). He taught that the natural aim and highest good of man was pleasure or 'an independent and peaceful state of body and mind' and defined philosophy as the attempt to gain happiness by means of discussion and reasoning.

Erymanthian Boar, a savage animal that was supposed to have ranged Mount Erymanthus in Arcadia until killed by Hercules.

Evander, a mythological minor deity who settled on the site of Rome. Hercules visited him and killed the monster Cacus who had ravaged Evander's land. See note p. 146 and Virgil, *Aen.*, 8, 185 ff.

Euripides, Greek tragedian (*c.*485–*c.*406 B.C.).

Eurydice, the wife of Orpheus.

Fabricius Luscinus, Gaius, Roman general and politician (third century B.C.). He was a byword for the austerity and incorruptibility typical of ancient Roman virtue.

Franks, the name assumed by a coalition of German tribes on the middle and lower Rhine who overran Gaul in the course of the fifth century. Under Clovis they destroyed the last vestiges of Roman power there and laid the foundations of the later kingdom of France.

Furies, mythological spirits of punishment.

Gaudentius, a discredited informer, otherwise unknown, who laid information against Boethius.

Gundobad (Gundebadus), Arian king of the Burgundians (*c.* A.D. 480–516). His son married a daughter of Theodoric and his niece became the wife of Clovis.

Hercules, mythological Greek hero famous for his strength and courage. See note pp. 145–6.

Hermes, the Arcadian God who came to the aid of Odysseus in dealing with Circe. See note p. 126.

Hermus, an auriferous river in Turkey (modern Gediz).

Hesperides, the mythological guardians along with the dragon Ladon of the golden apples given to Hera at her marriage with Zeus and which Hercules was set to win as his eleventh labour.

Homer, the Greek epic poet (sometime before 700 B.C.).

Horace (Quintus Horatius Flaccus), Roman poet (65–8 B.C.).

Hydra, the water-serpent killed by Hercules at Lerna in Argolis; it had nine heads, and as fast as one of them was cut off, two more sprang up in its place.

Iamblichus, Neoplatonist philosopher (*c.* A.D. 250–*c.* 325). He was born in Coele Syria, studied under Porphyry in Rome or Sicily, wrote on Pythagoras and composed an anthology of earlier writers. He was credited with important contributions to the development of the philosophy of Plotinus, but in fact his works are superficial and substitute theosophy and magic for the mysticism of Plotinus.

Indus, a river flowing into the Arabian Sea through what is now modern Pakistan.

Ithaca, one of the Ionian Islands off the west coast of Greece, the home of Odysseus.

Ixion, according to Greek mythology he murdered his father-in-law. He was purified by Zeus but attempted to seduce the goddess Hera. As a punishment he was bound in Hades to an ever revolving wheel.

John I, saint and pope in succession to St Hormisdas (A.D. 523). He was sent by Theodoric on a mission to the Emperor at Constantinople, but on the confirmation of Theodoric's suspicions of the pro-Eastern party at Rome, was thrown into prison where he died in 526.

Justinian (Flavius Petrus Sabbatius Iustinianus), Roman Emperor of the East (A.D. 527–65). Through his general Belisarius he invaded and occupied Italy in the period after Theodoric's death. His political ambition to reunite the Eastern and Western Empire was probably the inspiration of the pro-Eastern circle around Symmachus and Boethius.

Juvenal (Decimus Iunius Iuvenalis), greatest of the Roman satiric poets (*c.* A.D. 50–after 127).

Liberius, a Roman minister of Odoacer and later of Theodoric, Praetorian Prefect 493–500. It is recorded that he was a wise and skilful administrator.

Lombards, an East Germanic people who invaded Italy in A.D. 568 not long after Justinian had re-established the imperial rule there.

Lucan (Marcus Annaeus Lucanus), Roman poet, author of the *Pharsalia,* a poem in ten books about the civil war between Caesar and Pompey (A.D. 39–65).

Lynceus, a mythological Greek hero endowed with supernatural sharpness of sight.

Martianus Capella, author of a long encyclopedic mixture of verse and prose called *The Marriage of Mercury and Philology* (early fifth century A.D.). The form of this work (Menippean satire) may have influenced Boethius but not its whimsical and pedantic subject matter or 'perversely mannered' style. The work of Martianus was widely appreciated in the Middle Ages.

Menander, Greek comic playwright (342/1–291/90 B.C.).

Monophysites, a heretical sect which taught that in the Person of the incarnate Christ there was a single divine nature: the orthodox teaching is that there is a double nature in Christ, divine and human.

Muses, Greek goddesses of poetry, music and dance. The later addition of Muses of astronomy, philosophy and all intellectual pursuits provides Dame Philosophy with the muses she opposes to those she finds at Boethius' bedside in I, 1.

Nearchus, a Greek Tyrant: see Zeno of Elea.

Nemea, a valley on the north borders of Argolis, the scene of Hercules' fight with the lion. See note p. 146.

Neoplatonism, the revival of Platonism which reached its peak in the third century A.D. It was really a new synthesis of elements from Platonism, Aristotelianism, Pythagoreanism and Stoicism. It survived until the closing of the pagan schools by Justinian in 529 and deeply influenced Christian thought in the Middle Ages and the Renaissance. The chief Neoplatonist philosophers were Plotinus and his pupil Porphyry.

Nero (Nero Claudius Caesar), Roman Emperor (A.D. 37–68). He was reputed to have arranged the murder of his stepbrother Britannicus (who had a better claim to the throne) and of his mother Agrippina.

Nicocreon, a tyrant of Salamis in Cyprus (ruled 332/1–311/10 B.C.). The philosopher Anaxarchus of Abdera is said to have caused him mortal offence in the course of a drinking bout, and when he fell into the tyrant's hands in 323 he was pounded to death in a mortar.

Nominalism, the name given to the medieval school of philosophy which 'held that universals were merely words, that only individuals existed, and that the genus or the species corresponded to nothing in the real world' (G. Leff).

Nonius, unknown Roman politician satirized by Catullus. See note p. 85.

Odoacer, a Hunnish king of Italy, murdered by Theodoric (c. A.D. 433–493).

Odysseus, mythological king of Ithaca, and one of the leaders of the Greek expedition to Troy. He is the hero of the *Odyssey* in which his adventures on the return voyage from Troy are recounted.

Opilio, younger brother of Cyprian. He fell from favour under Theodoric but regained his position by laying information against Boethius. Under Theodoric's grandson Athalaric he held high office as Count of the Sacred Largesses (527 A.D.) and ambassador with Liberius to Constantinople.

Orpheus, famous mythological Greek musician reputed to be able to move trees and charm wild animals. He went down to Hades to recover his dead wife. See p. 113.

Ostrogoths, the eastern group of the Germanic peoples called Goths, settled in the third century A.D. in the steppelands between the Crimea and the rivers Don and Dniester. The sudden irruption of the Asiatic Huns caused them to move and eventually settle in the Po valley in Italy. They were Arian Christians.

Ovid (Publius Ovidius Naso), Roman poet (43 B.C.–?A.D. 17).

Papinian (Aemilius Papinianus), Roman jurist executed in A.D. 212 on the orders of the emperor Caracalla for disapproving of the murder of the Emperor's brother Geta.

Parmenides, Greek poet and philosopher at Athens (c. 450 B.C.).

Parthians, a semi-nomadic people between the Euphrates and the Indus, traditional enemies of Rome, famous for their horsemanship.

Paulinus, a Roman of consular rank defended by Boethius against the rapacity of the Goths. He is possibly the Paulinus who was consul in 493 and prosecuted by Symmachus and Festus (*Variae* 1, 23); but Boethius would hardly have referred to Symmachus as a 'palace jackal.' Paulinus is spoken of with approval by Cassiodorus in another letter (2, 3).

Paulus (Lucius Aemilius Paulus Macedonicus), Roman general and administrator, consul 182 and 168 B.C., conqueror of Macedonia. See p. 57.

Perses (or *Perseus*), last king of Macedonia, 179–168 B.C. He was defeated and captured by Aemilius Paulus and led in triumph through Rome. See p. 58 and Livy XLV, 7 ff.

Phoebus, the sun god. See note p. 118. Brother of *Phoebe* or *Luna*, the moon goddess.

Pholoe, a mountain south east of Elis where Hercules was reputed to have visited the centaur Pholus. He was attacked by a band of centaurs whom he put to flight. See note p. 146. Pholus was accidentally killed and buried in the mountain which was named after him.

Plato, the Athenian philosopher (*c.*429–347 B.C.). He taught near the grove of Academus, whence the school he founded to train men for the service of the state was called the Academy: it survived to A.D. 529.

Plotinus, Neoplatonist Greek philosopher (A.D. 205–269/70). He studied under Ammonius Saccas at Alexandria and taught at Rome. His philosophical essays, the *Enneads*, were collected and arranged by his pupil Porphyry. E. R. Dodds calls him 'the most powerful philosophical mind between Aristotle and Aquinas'.

Polyphemus, a Cyclops blinded by Odysseus. See note p. 145 and Homer, *Od.*, IX.

Pompey (Gnaeus Pompeius), Roman general and politician, one time colleague and later enemy of Caesar (106–48 B.C.). His struggle with Caesar culminating in his defeat at Pharsalus and murder in Egypt is the subject of Lucan's *Pharsalia*.

Porphyry (Porphyrius), scholar, philosopher and student of religions (A.D. 232/3–*c.*305). He was the devoted personal disciple of Plotinus whose writings he edited. Among his many works (now partly lost) were numerous philosophical commentaries on Plato, Aristotle and others, including the famous *Isagoge* or *Introduction to the Categories of Aristotle*, which became a standard medieval textbook of logic and was translated and commented on by Boethius. He was a remarkable polymath, but his work as a thinker was not important.

Proclus, Neoplatonic Greek philosopher and head of the Academy (A.D. 412–485).

Pseudo-Dionysius, the name given to an unknown mystical theologian of *c.* A.D. 500, who seems to have aimed at making a synthesis of Neoplatonist thought and Christian teaching. He writes of the mystical union of the soul with God achieved by the process of 'unknowing' in which the soul leaves behind the knowledge of the senses and the reason to be illuminated and deified by God. His writings exercised a profound influence on medieval religious experience.

Ptolemy (Claudius Ptolemaeus) of Alexandria, Greek geographer (*fl.* A.D. 121–151). He wrote on trigonometry, astronomy, optics and geography; the last is an eight book treatise and atlas which despite its faults remained the standard geography until relatively recent times.

Pythagoras, early Greek astronomer, mathematician and religious leader (sixth century B.C.).

Ravenna, a city on the Adriatic coast of Italy, capital of the Western Empire from the beginning of the fifth century.

Realists, the name of the school of medieval philosophy which in contradistinction to the Nominalists 'recognized, in some degree, the existence of genera and species and their correspondence to reality' (G. Leff).

Regulus, Marcus Atilius, Roman general (third century B.C.). In 255 he was defeated and captured by the Carthaginians, and was later sent on parole to Rome to arrange an exchange of prisoners. The (probably apocryphal) story of his voluntary return to Carthage and death by torture became a famous episode in the annals of Roman history. See Horace *Odes* 3, 5 and Cicero *De Officiis* 3, 26, 99.

Rusticiana, daughter of Symmachus and wife of Boethius.

Saturn, the planet. See note p. 118.

Seneca, Lucius Annaeus, distinguished and wealthy Roman orator, philosopher and tragedian, tutor and later adviser of the Emperor Nero (*c.*5/4 B.C.–A.D. 65). When he was nearly seventy Seneca attempted to retire and give up his immense wealth to Nero, but the Emperor refused. Later he was implicated in a plot against Nero and forced to commit suicide.

Sidonius (Gaius Sollius Modestus Apollinaris), saint, statesman, author and bishop of Clermont. He was a Gallo-Roman born at Lyons of noble family about A.D. 430, and was Prefect of Rome 468–9. His appointment as bishop (while he was probably still a layman) was political, but he abandoned poetry, became a benefactor of monks and gave away his wealth. He was one of the last representatives of classical culture and his poetry was skilful if uninspired.

Socrates, the Greek philosopher (469–399 B.C.). He was arrested and tried on a charge of corrupting the young and being guilty of impiety. Thirty days elapsed between his condemnation and death by drinking hemlock, and his conversations during this period are preserved by Plato. See *The Last Days of Socrates* translated by Hugh Tredennick. (Penguin Classics, 1954.)

Sophocles, Greek tragedian (*c*.496–406 B.C.).

Soranus, Marcus Barea, a prominent Roman of the time of Nero, who had been a just and energetic governor of Asia. He was forced to commit suicide by Nero (Tacitus, *Annals*, 16, 32).

Statius, Publius Papinius, Roman poet (A.D. 45–96). He wrote occasional poems (the *Silvae*) and two epics (the *Thebais* and *Achilleis*), the latter interrupted by his death. In his fluent and highly polished verse he imitated Virgil.

Stoicism, a philosophical school founded by Zeno of Citium *c*.300 B.C. See note p. 159. Its ethical system and teaching concerning the virtuous life were very influential; Seneca was one of the chief stoics under the emperors, and Stoicism provided the philosophical basis for the opposition to imperial autocracy. The influence of Stoicism on later Neoplatonism and on some fathers of the Christian church was considerable.

Stymphalus, lake and district in North East Arcadia (modern Zaraká). Pausanias describes a temple of Artemis there near which stood some statues of young women with legs and thighs of birds. These are the legendary Stymphalian birds whose destruction was one of the labours of Hercules. See note p. 146.

Symmachus, Quintus Aurelius Memmius, Roman consul (A.D. 485), patrician, and head of the Senate (A.D. 524). He is spoken of with affection and admiration by his son-in-law, Boethius, and praised by Ennodius and Cassiodorus. He combined the interests of philosopher and historian (writing a Roman history in seven books) and was an orator of considerable eloquence. He spent money on the repair of public buildings in Rome and impressed his contemporaries with his love of the Roman ideal. Cassiodorus calls him 'a modern imitator of the ancient Cato, but [he] surpassed the virtues of the men of old in [his love of] the most holy religion'; although he served Theodoric, his ancestry and upbringing led him to oppose him both as a heretic and a barbarian. He was executed in 525.

Tagus, one of the principal rivers of Spain (modern Tajo) celebrated for its fish, oysters and gold-bearing sand.

Tantalus, mythological king of Lydia whose crime – either the devouring of his own children or theft of food from the gods – was punished in Hades as follows. He was tormented by hunger and thirst, and tantalized by being placed in water up to his chin and with fruit hanging over his head; but whenever he moved to eat or drink the fruit and water receded. See p. 114.

Theodoric, known as Theodoric the Great and remembered in saga as Dietrich von Bern (Verona). He was king of the Ostrogoths in succession to his father Theudemir who d. A.D. 474. Theodoric was born about 454 and sent at the age of seven as a hostage to Constantinople where he received his early upbringing and education. He led his people on various campaigns both for and against the Emperor (who at various stages adopted him and made him consul), and eventually set out for Italy with the blessing of Constantinople in 488. Ravenna surrendered in 493 and after the murder of Odoacer Theodoric became king of Italy. His rule brought peace and prosperity which was only broken by the resumption of the persecution of Arians in the east and the discovery of treason among the senators in Rome. He died with his policy in ruins in 526.

Thulé, an island in the Northern Ocean regarded as the most northerly point of the known world, variously identified as Mainland in the Shetland Islands or Iceland.

Tiresias, a legendary blind Theban seer.

Tityus, a mythological giant punished in Hades for assaulting a goddess. He lay stretched out on the ground covering nine acres while two vultures tore at his liver. See note p. 115.

Triguilla, a Goth whose evil designs were frustrated by Boethius. Their nature is not specified and nothing more is known of him except that he was a palace official.

Troy, a city in modern Turkey near the Aegean entrance to the Dardanelles (modern Hissarlik). It was the scene of the Trojan war in the *Iliad*.

Tully, see *Cicero*.

Tyrian Dyes, so called from Tyre, an important city on the coast of Phoenicia south of Sidon, famous as the seat of a purple-dyeing industry.

Verona, an important city in Northern Italy near lake Garda, used as an occasional capital by Theodoric.

Vesuvius, the famous volcano in central Italy near Naples which engulfed Pompeii and Herculaneum in A.D. 79.

Virgil (Publius Vergilius Maro), greatest of all the Roman poets and author of the *Aeneid* (70–19 B.C.).

Zeno, Roman Emperor of the East (A.D. *c.*450–91). His reign was largely a succession of disastrous wars against various enemies including the Ostrogoths. He was author of the *Henoticon:* see under *Acacius*.

Zeno of *Citium*, Greek philosopher and founder of the Stoic school (335–263 B.C.).

Zeno of *Elea*, Greek philosopher, pupil and friend of Parmenides, b. *c.*490 B.C. He was a member of the Eleatic school of philosophy and one of three philosophers of whom Diogenes Laertius tells the story that he bit out his own tongue to scorn the tyrant (in Zeno's case called Nearchus) who was torturing him into confession: he was afterwards pounded to death in a mortar.

FOR THE BEST IN PAPERBACKS, LOOK FOR THE

In every corner of the world, on every subject under the sun, Penguin represents quality and variety – the very best in publishing today.

For complete information about books available from Penguin – including Pelicans, Puffins, Peregrines and Penguin Classics – and how to order them, write to us at the appropriate address below. Please note that for copyright reasons the selection of books varies from country to country.

In the United Kingdom: For a complete list of books available from Penguin in the U.K., please write to *Dept E.P., Penguin Books Ltd, Harmondsworth, Middlesex, UB7 0DA*

In the United States: For a complete list of books available from Penguin in the U.S., please write to *Dept BA, Penguin, 299 Murray Hill Parkway, East Rutherford, New Jersey 07073*

In Canada: For a complete list of books available from Penguin in Canada, please write to *Penguin Books Canada Ltd, 2801 John Street, Markham, Ontario L3R 1B4*

In Australia: For a complete list of books available from Penguin in Australia, please write to the *Marketing Department, Penguin Books Australia Ltd, P.O. Box 257, Ringwood, Victoria 3134*

In New Zealand: For a complete list of books available from Penguin in New Zealand, please write to the *Marketing Department, Penguin Books (NZ) Ltd, Private Bag, Takapuna, Auckland 9*

In India: For a complete list of books available from Penguin, please write to *Penguin Overseas Ltd, 706 Eros Apartments, 56 Nehru Place, New Delhi, 110019*

In Holland: For a complete list of books available from Penguin in Holland, please write to *Penguin Books Nederland B.V., Postbus 195, NL–1380AD Weesp, Netherlands*

In Germany: For a complete list of books available from Penguin, please write to *Penguin Books Ltd, Friedrichstrasse 10 – 12, D–6000 Frankfurt Main 1, Federal Republic of Germany*

In Spain: For a complete list of books available from Penguin in Spain, please write to *Longman Penguin España, Calle San Nicolas 15, E–28013 Madrid, Spain*

A CHOICE OF PENGUINS AND PELICANS

Lateral Thinking for Management   Edward de Bono

Creativity and lateral thinking can work together for managers in developing new products or ideas; Edward de Bono shows how.

Understanding Organizations   Charles B. Handy

Of practical as well as theoretical interest, this book shows how general concepts can help solve specific organizational problems.

The Art of Japanese Management   Richard Tanner Pascale and Anthony G. Athos   With an Introduction by Sir Peter Parker

Japanese industrial success owes much to Japanese management techniques, which we in the West neglect at our peril. The lessons are set out in this important book.

My Years with General Motors   Alfred P. Sloan   With an Introduction by John Egan

A business classic by the man who took General Motors to the top – and kept them there for decades.

Introducing Management   Ken Elliott and Peter Lawrence (eds.)

An important and comprehensive collection of texts on modern management which draw some provocative conclusions.

English Culture and the Decline of the Industrial Spirit   Martin J. Wiener

A major analysis of why the 'world's first industrial nation has never been comfortable with industrialism'. 'Very persuasive' – Anthony Sampson in the *Observer*